T0343930

RONT

EDITOR'S LETTER

Holding the rich and powerful to account

Editor **MARTIN BRIGHT** says whistleblowers are extraordinary people but they often pay a terrible personal price

THE IMPORTANCE OF the role of whistleblowers in exposing corruption and malpractice is well-established in law and rightly celebrated in a string of Hollywood movies from All the President's Men to Erin Brockovich. But whistleblowers should also be celebrated as champions of free expression. The Summer 2021 edition of Index on Censorship highlights several prominent cases around the world. Brittany Winner writes exclusively about her sister, Reality, the former US intelligence specialist who leaked details of Russian interference in the 2016 American election. Winner was recently released from prison but is still prohibited from talking about the case. Her family is campaigning for a full pardon.

As an investigative journalist, I have worked with several high-profile examples, including Iraq War whistleblower Katharine Gun, the subject of the recent movie, Official Secrets, starring Keira Knightley. I know from personal experience that whistleblowers are extraordinary people, who take incredible risks to bring the rich and powerful to account. This often exacts a terrible personal price, with whistleblowers losing their livelihoods, their mental health and even their freedom.

For this issue of Index, I have examined the case of the case of Jonathan Taylor, an oil industry whistleblower who revealed a multimillion-dollar bribe network stretching from Angola and Equatorial Guinea to Iraq and Brazil. Taylor is currently stranded in Croatia awaiting extradition to Monaco, the home of the company he exposed. Index associate editor Mark Frary interviews possibly the most famous whistleblower of

them all, Daniel Ellsberg, on the 50th anniversary of the Pentagon Papers, which exposed the secret history of American involvement in Vietnam.

The issue also contains an exclusive interview with playwright and long-time Index supporter Tom Stoppard, Nerma Jelacic writes about how misinformation has become part of how the world sees the Syrian conflict and veteran correspondent Henry Macdonald on attacks on press freedom in Northern Ireland.

Over recent months, Index has been closely involved with the case of Maya Forstater, a woman who lost her job at a think tank after expressing her view that people cannot change their biological sex. Index intervened in her employment tribunal on free speech grounds, arguing that her gender critical views were protected under equality legislation. However, we recognise this is a controversial case that demands further discussion. We have therefore commissioned two writers to give their views about the case. Philosopher Kathleen Stock hails the judgement as a victory for free speech, while Phoenix Andrews worries about its implications for trans people. ✖

Martin Bright is editor of Index on Censorship

50(02):01/01|DOI:10.1177/03064220211033779

Watching Eyes

MARK FRARY introduces our cover artist Tatiana Zelenskaya

Tatiana Zelenskaya was born and grew up in Bishkek, the capital of Kyrgyzstan and studied art at the National Academy of Arts of the Kyrgyz Republic. She majored in industrial graphics, but prefers to work in a more creative direction: illustration, animations, posters and contemporary art. Zelenskaya's work regularly covers themes such as feminism, violence and human rights and in March 2020, she was arrested for taking part in a women's rights protest in the country. She has beenshortlisted for an Index 2021 Freedom of Expression Award.

LEFT: The artist Tatyana Zelenskaya

CONTENTS

The Index

A round-up of events in the world of free expression from Index's unparalleled network of writers and activists. Edited by **MARK FRARY**

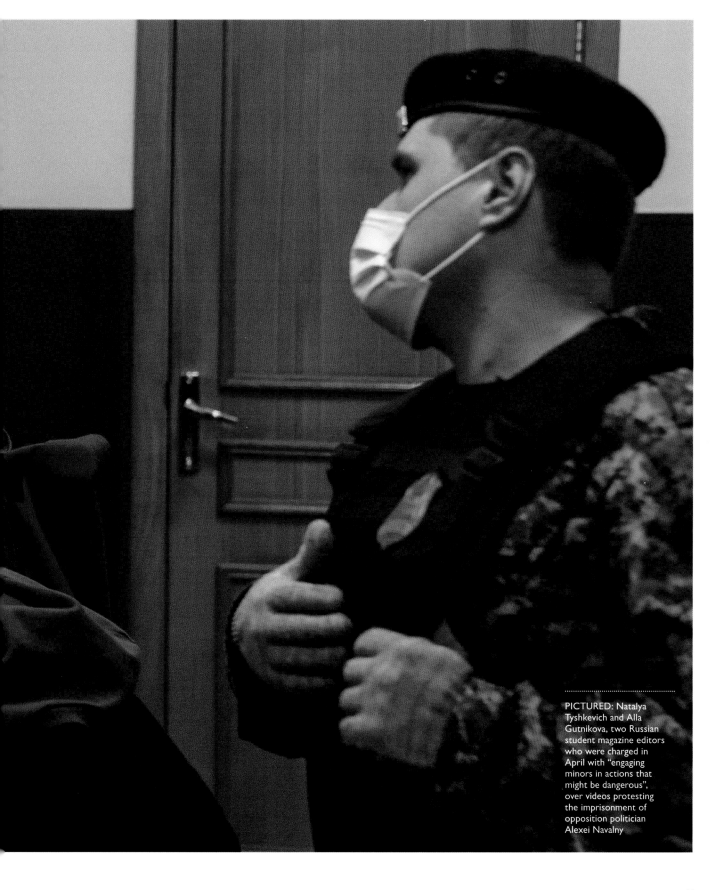

PICTURED: Natalya Tyshkevich and Alla Gutnikova, two Russian student magazine editors who were charged in April with "engaging minors in actions that might be dangerous", over videos protesting the imprisonment of opposition politician Alexei Navalny

The Index

A VERY TOUGH MENTOR

MY INSPIRATION

NATALIA TYSHKEVICH, a student journalist who has been placed under house arrest for participating in a video about freedom of expression, describes how the feminist activist and researcher **NADIA PLUNGIAN** shaped her views

THE WOMAN WHO is my inspiration is the most difficult friend I've ever had and the toughest mentor. But looking back I see now that she helped propel me out of the academic world into media activism. I met feminist activist Nadia Plungian during the summer I graduated from the Moscow 57th School, considered to be one of the best schools in Moscow. Nadia was a well-known figure within Russia's feminist community. She was also an alumna of my school, and she had a strong position against the sexual abuse that had been happening there for years.

In September 2016, that situation became public and exploded into a vast media scandal, much discussed on

> Nadia was a well-known figure within Russia's feminist community...and she had a strong position against the sexual abuse that had been happening there for years

ABOVE: Russian feminist activist Nadia Plungian

Russian social networks and in media such as Meduza and BBC Russia. However, student voices were absent from the conversation. I interviewed my schoolmates who were survivors of sexual abuse, but only for an internal investigation that was never finished. We trusted neither the school administration nor journalists.

We needed a different type of approach. We started meeting Nadia to discuss the issues of gender and social practices in the post-Soviet context. The comparison of contemporary society with the Soviet one gave me an understanding of where the institutional control and the prohibition of criticism came from.

For years, Nadia existed in different worlds – academic, artistic and activist, experimenting with all these fields, provoking new situations. She was a

CREDIT: Natalia Tyshkevich/ Ivan Vodopjanov/Kommersand/Sipa USA; (Nadia Plungian) Valerij Ledenev/Flickr

Free speech in numbers

107

The number of people arrested in London during so-called Kill the Bill demonstrations against UK government plans to increase police powers

2.5MILLION

The number of followers on Weibo of popular blogger Qiu Ziming, who has been jailed for eight months for questioning the Chinese death toll in Indian border clashes in 2020

25

The number of vexatious lawsuits still active against Maltese investigative journalist Daphne Caruana Galizia, who was murdered in 2017

78%

The percentage of convictions against journalists in Turkey in 2020 which were for alleged terrorism-related offences historian of Soviet art, an art curator, a poet, an artist, an activist, a philosopher and, eventually, she became a media manager. She started curating the art section at the Colta.ru platform, inviting contemporary artists, writers and cultural critics to contribute. All of them were strictly evaluated before being accepted. Were they artistic enough? Were they intellectual enough? Were they independent enough? Although I did publish my research on neo-modernism there, I didn't pass the evaluation.

Suddenly I found myself expelled from Nadia's circle because I dared to disagree with her vision. It made me stop my public activity. I started doing all the work not in my own name but in the name of the student journal where I volunteered, Doxa, organising events. Doxa gave me a kind of shelter, where I could process ideas such as post-colonial thought or structural violence that I learned in academia and in Nadia's circle, but without the snobbish intellectual pressure. It was a kind of relief. I found like-minded people with whom I am currently writing papers on social topics, including harassment in Russian academia. ✖

Natalia Tyshkevich is a Moscow-based cyberfeminist, historian and activist, working at the textile archives and at student journal Doxa. On 14 April the police knocked on the door of her home to conduct a search. Police also raided the flats of her three Doxa colleagues, Armen Aramyan, Vladimir Metelkin and Alla Gutnikova, as well as those of her parents and Gutnikova's parents, and the Doxa office. The four Doxa workers are accused of participating in a video about young people defending their rights. They now are under house arrest and forbidden to go online

Correction

Remembering Rex Cornelio
VOL. 49 NO. 4
In the winter 2020 edition of Index, we published a story on the murder of Rex Cornelio, a radio journalist in the Philippines. We would like to make it clear that in a 2017 libel case involving Cornelio, judge Catherine Dato acquitted the journalist rather than dismissing the case against him. ✖

You may have missed

BENJAMIN LYNCH rounds up important news on free expression from around the world

Sickening threat to journalist
PATRICIA DEVLIN'S FAMILY IS TARGETED
Northern Ireland journalist Patricia Devlin, who wrote for the spring issue of Index, received an appalling message from someone on social media threatening to rape her child. Devlin has reported extensively on the actions of paramilitary organisations in Belfast and Northern Ireland and has received many threats before. This is the second threat of rape. Read more in our feature on p30.

Six-and-a-half years for blogging
UZBEKISTAN'S POOR RECORD CONTINUES

Uzbek YouTuber Otabek Sattoryi was sentenced to six-and-a-half years in jail after being convicted of "libel and large-scale extortion".
Sattoryi is the founder of YouTube channel Xalq Fikri, known to be effective in uncovering widescale corruption at a local level. He was arrested on 29 January before his eventual conviction on 10 May. Reporters Without Borders said the charges against him were "baseless".

Belarusian journalist detained after plane diversion
INTERNATIONAL OUTCRY OVER UNPRECEDENTED ARREST
Belarusian authorities recorded a false bomb threat to Ryanair flight FR4978 on 23 May to ensure the capture and arrest of dissident journalist Roman Protasevich, who co-founded the opposition Telegram channel Nexta.
The plane departed Athens and was destined for Lithuania before it was intercepted in Belarusian airspace and forced to land in the capital, Minsk.
Protasevich has since appeared in a "confession" video released on state TV, but questions over his physical condition remain. He was arrested along with his Russian girlfriend Sofia Sapega.

US journalist detained in Myanmar
FURTHER ATTACKS ON JOURNALISTS
American reporter Danny Fenster is being held in Myanmar's notorious Insein prison after being arrested at Yangon International Airport on 24 May as he tried to leave the city. He faces a three-year sentence.
Fenster is managing editor of news site Frontier Myanmar, which has reported on the severe civil unrest in the country ever since the military coup on 1 February.
At the time of publication, 85 journalists in Myanmar have been arrested, 38 of whom are still detained. ✖

The Index

PEOPLE WATCH

JESSICA NÍ MHAINÍN highlights the stories of journalists imprisoned in Bangladesh and Algeria, a missing Rwandan poet, and a Brazilian academic facing a defamation lawsuit

Rozina Islam

HUMAN RIGHTS DEFENDER AND JOURNALIST – BANGLADESH

The award-winning Bangladeshi investigative journalist and human rights defender is currently being detained for allegedly collecting and photographing sensitive government documents. If charged and convicted, she faces up to 14 years in prison or the death penalty. Islam like others has been targeted by the Bangladeshi authorities for criticising their handling of the pandemic.

Conrado Hübner Mendes

ACADEMIC – BRAZIL

The São Paolo law professor and newspaper columnist has been a critic of president Jair Bolsonaro but Brazil's attorney-general is now attempting to silence Mendes. On 19 May, Augusto Aras filed a criminal defamation lawsuit against him. He has also filed a petition to the ethics committee of Mendes's university. More than 80 professors from around the world have signed a statement in his defence.

Jamila Loukil

JOURNALIST AND HUMAN RIGHTS DEFENDER – ALGERIA

The journalist and member of the Algerian League for the Defence of Human Rights is one of 15 Hirak (an Algerian pro-democracy movement) activists currently facing up to 20 years in prison or the death penalty for alleged "participation in a terrorist movement" and "conspiracy against the state". Algeria's Penal Code was amended on 8 June to expand the definition of terrorism.

Innocent Bahati

POET – RWANDA

The poet, known for his writings about repression, human rights abuses and poverty in Rwanda, remains missing several months after his disappearance on 7 February. He failed to return after going to a hotel to meet someone. His phones remains switched off. Human rights organisations have expressed concern that Bahati is a victim of enforced disappearances, which are startlingly common in the country. ✖

Investigative journalism under attack

DREW SULLIVAN, publisher and co-founder of the Organised Crime and Corruption Reporting Project (OCCRP), says investigative journalism is giving corrupt governments something to fear

Two investigative journalists in the OCCRP network were recently targeted for their reporting. Stevan Dojčinović, from our Serbian member centre KRIK, was the victim of a government-supported media smear campaign that cast him as an ally of a brutal drug gang.

And Roman Anin, of our Russian member centre, IStories, had his apartment and office raided and was interrogated by the FSB over a years-old investigation he carried out into a yacht owned by a powerful associate of Vladimir Putin for which his newspaper was successfully sued by Rosneft head Igor Sechin.

It's not a coincidence that Stevan and Roman are among the best investigative reporters in their countries who have been exposing wrongdoing by the powerful for years.

The increasingly harsh media crackdowns spreading around the world like a disease are a response, in part, to the growing impact of investigative journalism. Reporters have become very effective at exposing autocrats' criminal and corrupt activities. OCCRP (**occrp.org**) works with journalists at many independent media outlets around the world on cross-border investigations. We also provide critical resources such as digital and physical security and pro bono legal assistance. We'll keep working and supporting journalists in our global network such as Stevan and Roman so they can keep doing their work and informing the public. ✖

BRITAIN'S PROTEST POLICING IN FOCUS

Another look at the biggest story from the last quarter. Keep up to date at **INDEXONCENSORSHIP.ORG**

Sarah Everard's death led to public protests despite Covid

The murder of marketing executive Sarah Everard in London in March 2021 brought freedom of expression to the fore.

The UK was in national lockdown but people felt compelled to take to the streets to protest – one of our fundamental rights, even in times of pandemic.

Writing in Index in the aftermath of Everard's death, MP Jess Phillips said that censorship was at the heart of violence against women and girls.

She wrote: "Without curtailing the freedom of a woman's speech, you cannot curtail her physical and sexual freedoms. Every perpetrator knows that you must convince a victim that if she speaks things will get worse."

They say things such as "They will take the children off you if you tell anyone" or "If you say anything, I will have you deported".

Phillips added: "The outpouring of grief by women in the wake of the death of Sarah Everard is not just because of our sorrow at her loss and the loss of all the other 119 women who [died] at the hands of a violent man in the last year.

"The case of the killing of Sarah Everard has reminded women that we have been self-censoring on behalf of society who didn't want to hear about our fears and our pain. We have been putting on a face."

Read the story: **tinyurl.com/Index502everard**

Impartiality and independence of police watchdog questioned

An author of a government report into the handling of public protests has expressed her serious concerns about the independence and impartiality of the police watchdog. The report from Her Majesty's Inspectorate of Constabulary looked at policing in the wake of the Black Lives Matter and Extinction Rebellion protests and backed Home Office proposals for tightening up the law. The Police, Crime, Sentencing and Courts Bill which followed sparked protests across the country.

Alice O'Keeffe, who worked as an associate editor at the HMIC, feared the conclusions may have contributed to the crackdown on the vigil for Sarah Everard on Clapham Common in south London. The 33-year-old's killing provoked a national outcry in the UK about violence against women. Ms O'Keeffe was removed from the team tasked by Home Secretary Priti Patel to report on the policing of the vigil itself after she expressed her view that the "handling of the vigil was completely unacceptable and disproportionate."

In its report, the HMIC concluded the police acted appropriately in handcuffing and arresting women protestors at the vigil, although it recognised coverage in the media had been a public relations disaster.

In a letter to HMIC head Sir Tom Winsor, seen by Index on Censorship, the civil servant raised her "serious and urgent concerns about breaches of the civil service code". The letter makes a number of serious claims about the impartiality of the inspectorate, including claims of a lack of diversity, that the inspectorate had not considered the threat from extreme-right wing groups and demonstrated consistent bias against peaceful protest groups, drawing comparisons between them and the IRA.

Read the story: **tinyurl.com/Index502policing** ✖

The Index

World In Focus: Belarus

Alexander Lukashenko's crackdown on peaceful protest and the media has continued, the most notable of which was the forced grounding of a plane carrying journalist and activist Roman Protasevich. But incidents have happened elsewhere in the country too.

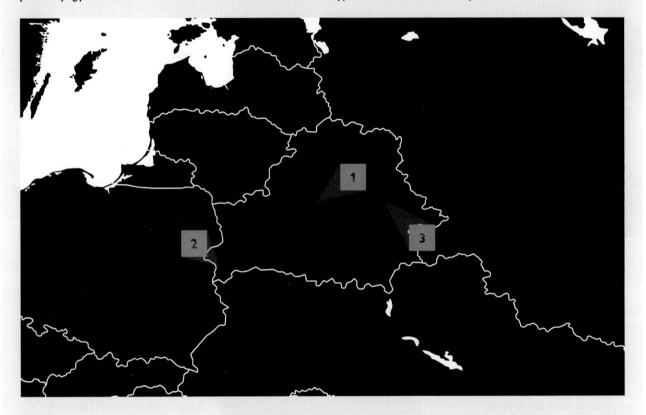

1 Minsk

Belarus's Ministry of Information has blocked access to probono.by, a human rights support website set up in August 2020 after the disupted re-election of President Alexander Lukashenko.

The site aims to help those affected by the subsequent protests and Lukashenko's crackdown by connecting victims to lawyers and helping with the searches for loved ones who have been arrested. It includes information on lawyers and gives medical and mental health advice.

Probono.by was hosted on servers in Belarus but it has now been moved to allow access via VPN or from abroad.

2 Brest/Hrodna

Tut.by, one of the country's most popular news sites, was shut down in May, denying access to those within Belarus and outside. Its offices in Brest and Hrodna as well as in the capital were raided, along with the home of editor Marina Zolotova on 18 May.

Several of Tut.by's journalists had already been targeted, including Katerina Borisevich, who was given a six-month sentence on 2 March although she was released on 19 May. Her colleague Lyubov Kasperovich was arrested on 17 May.

The government's Financial Investigations Department claimed the raids were based on "suspected tax evasion".

3 Mahilyow (Mogilev)

Deutsche Welle journalist Alyksandr Burakou and 6tv.by reporter Uladzimir Laptsevich were covering a trial of political prisoners when arrested on 12 May.

They were made to strip naked after their arrests outside court. Burakou claimed he was subjected to regular cell searches, being forced to stay awake for several nights during detention. Both journalists went on hunger strike in protest at their treatment.

There have been well over 100 noted cases of torture by Lukashenko's authorities since protests erupted after the presidential election in August 2020. Many of the cases are said to be journalists. ✖

TECH WATCH: NFT

MARK FRARY looks at innovations with censorship and free speech implications

CAN'T HAVE BEEN the only one reaching for a dictionary to look up the word "fungible" recently. The word crops up in the term "non-fungible token", or NFT.

NFTs have created a stir in the art world by being used as a digital way to represent a one-of-kind work of art, also in digital form, such as an original digital photo or a music track. The ownership of the NFT signifies your ownership of the original digital asset, even if it has subsequently been copied and distributed.

It does this through the blockchain, the same technology that is used to authenticate transactions using cryptocurrencies such as Bitcoin, a sort of digital ledger that acts as an incorruptible source of truth about transactions and ownership.

Artists and collectors are recognising that there is a lucrative market in NFTs.

Even the creators of famous internet memes are cashing in, such as Zoë Roth who, as a young girl, featured in the 2005 meme Disaster Girl; an NFT representing the image of her in front of a burning building recently sold for almost half a million dollars.

On 16 April, an NFT representing an artwork combining a landmark court decision ruling the National Security Agency's mass surveillance violated the law with an iconic portrait of Edward Snowden by Platon went up for auction, with the proceeds going to the Freedom of the Press Foundation. It sold to a decentralised autonomous organisation, or DAO – a club of anonymous buyers – for $6,050,280.80 before fees.

NFTs are also being used to raise funds for organisations under threat. Some 80 Russian-speaking artists have put their works up for auction through the Rarible marketplace to raise funds for the independent Meduza news outlet.

Artists can also create controversial or critical works, sell them and receive the funds in cryptocurrency without the censors or authorities ever knowing. ✖

50(02):06/11|DOI:10.1177/03064220211033780

Ma Jian on China

To celebrate the launch of our spring issue which marked the 100th anniversary of the Chinese Communist Party, we held a virtual launch event with Index contributor and author Ma Jian. He read extracts of his most recent novel China Dream and was interviewed by journalist Tania Branigan. Ma said the world's governments courted danger by cosying up to the Chinese. He said: "When governments collaborate with totalitarian regimes committing atrocities, they grow richer, they get faster technology. But when they slowly discover that freedom of speech is growing smaller than this wealth, this technology is meaningless."

The world, he said, should look at Hong Kong.

"Hong Kong today is the rest of the world's tomorrow. It holds up a mirror to our future," he said.

But the author feels there is cause for optimism and that the CCP will not last forever. "The CCP will one day fall because it is not in tune with the values of humanity," he said. ✖

Watch the event: **tinyurl.com/ Index502majianlaunch**

CREDIT: Chris Ume

Ink spot: Malaysian press freedom

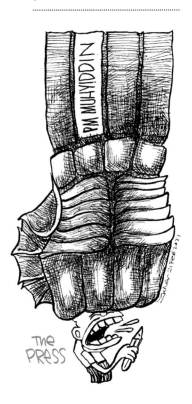

Zulkiflee Anwar Haque, better known as Zunar to Malaysians, is a political cartoonist who has been drawing cartoons for the past 20 years in Malaysia. His work exposes corruption and abuse of power committed by the government.

He has regularly been arrested and detained for alleged breaches of the country's Sedition Act and the Penal Code, and five of his cartoon books have been banned by the government.

This year, Malaysia dropped more places (18) than any other country on the Reporters Without Borders World Press Freedom Index to number 119, the subject of this issue's cartoon. ✖

Why journalists need emergency safe havens

Journalists tell Index how a new type of visa is vital to protect lives and stop media censorship. **RACHAEL JOLLEY** reports

LEFT: Amal Clooney speaking at the United Nations Security Council, 2019.

T HE NUMBER OF journalists killed while doing their work rose in 2020. It's no wonder, then, that a team of internationally acclaimed lawyers are advising governments to introduce emergency visas for reporters who have to flee for their lives when work becomes too dangerous.

The High Level Panel of Legal Experts on Media Freedom, a group of lawyers led by Amal Clooney and former president of the UK Supreme Court Lord Neuberger, has called for these visas to be made available quickly. The panel advises a coalition of 47 countries on how to prevent the erosion of media freedom, and how to hold to account those who harm journalists.

At the launch of the panel's report, Clooney said the current options open to journalists in danger were "almost without exception too lengthy to provide real protection". She added: "I would describe the bottom line as too few countries offer 'humanitarian' visas that could apply to journalists in danger as a result of their work."

The report that includes these recommendations was written by barrister Can Yeğinsu. It has been formally endorsed by the UN special rapporteur on the promotion and protection of the right to freedom of opinion and expression, the Inter-American Commission on Human Rights special rapporteur for freedom of expression, and the International Bar Association's Human Rights Institute.

As highlighted by the recent release of an International Federation of Journalists report showing 65 journalists and media workers were killed in 2020 – up 17 from 2019 – and 200 were jailed for their work, the issue is incredibly urgent.

Index has spoken to journalists who know what it is like to work in dangerous situations about why emergency visas are vital, and to the lawyer leading the charge to create them.

Syrian journalist Zaina Erhaim, who has worked for the BBC Arabic Service, has reported on her country's civil war. She believes part of the problem for journalists forced to flee because of their work is that many immigration systems are not set up to be reactive to those kinds of situations, "because the procedures for visas and immigration is so strict, and so slow and bureaucratic".

Erhaim, who grew up in Idlib in Syria's north-west, went on to report from rebel-held areas during the civil war, and she also trained citizen journalists.

The journalist, who won an Index award in 2016, has been threatened with death and harassed online. She moved to Turkey for her own safety and has spoken about not feeling safe to report on Syria at times, even from overseas, because of the threats.

She believes that until emergency visas are available quickly to those in urgent need, things will not change. "Until someone is finally able to act, journalists will either be in hiding, scared, assassinated or already imprisoned," she said.

"Many journalists don't even need to emigrate when they're being targeted or feel threatened. Some just need some peace for three or four months to put their mind together, and think what they've been through and decide whether they should come back or find another solution."

Erhaim, who currently lives in the UK, said it was also important to think about journalists' families.

Eritrean journalist Abraham Zere is living in exile in the USA after fleeing his country. He feels the visa proposal would offer journalists in challenging political situations some sense of hope. "It's so very important for local journalists to [be able to] flee their country from repressive regimes."

Eritrea is regularly labelled the worst country in the world for ➔

The procedures for visas and immigration is so strict, and so slow and bureaucratic

→ journalists, taking bottom position in RSF's World Press Freedom Index 2021, below North Korea. The RSF report highlights that 11 journalists are currently imprisoned in Eritrea without access to lawyers.

Zere said: "Until I left the country, for the last three years I was always prepared to be arrested. As a result of that constant fear, I abandoned writing. But if I were able to secure such a visa, I would have some sense of security."

Ryan Ho Kilpatrick is a journalist formerly based in Hong Kong who has recently moved to Taiwan. He has worked as an editor for the Hong Kong Free Press, as well as for the South China Morning Post, Time and The Wall Street Journal.

"I wasn't facing any immediate threats of violence, harassment, that sort of thing, [but] the environment for the journalists in Hong Kong was becoming a lot darker and a lot more dire, and [it was] a lot more difficult to operate there," he said.

He added that although his need to move wasn't because of threats, it had illustrated how difficult a relocation like that could be. "I tried applying from Hong Kong. I couldn't get a visa there. I then had to go halfway around the world to Canada to apply for a completely different visa there to get to Taiwan."

He feels the panel's recommendation is much needed. "Obviously, journalists around the world are facing politically motivated harassment or prosecution, or even violence or death. And [with] the framework as it is now, journalists don't really fit very neatly in it."

As far as the current situation for journalists in Hong Kong is concerned, he said: "It became a lot more dangerous reporting on protests in Hong Kong. It's immediate physical threats and facing tear gas, police and street clashes every day. The introduction of the national security law last year has made reporting a lot more difficult. Virtually overnight, sources are reluctant to speak to you,

even previously very vocal people, activists and lawyers."

In the few months since the panel launched its report and recommendations, no country has announced it will lead the way by offering emergency visas, but there are some promising signs from the likes of Canada, Germany and the Netherlands.

Report author Yeğinsu, who is part of the international legal team representing Rappler journalist Maria Ressa in the Philippines, is positive about the response, and believes that the new US president Joe Biden is giving global leadership on this issue. He said: "It is always the few that need to lead. It'll be interesting to see who does that."

However, he pointed out that journalists have become less safe in the months since the report's publication, with governments introducing laws during the pandemic that are being used aggressively against journalists.

Yeğinsu said the "recommendations are geared to really respond to instances

where there's a safety issue… so where the journalist is just looking for safe refuge". This could cover a few options, such as a temporary stay or respite before a journalist returns home.

The report puts into context how these emergency visas could be incorporated into immigration systems such as those in the USA, Canada, the EU and the UK, at low cost and without the need for massive changes.

One encouraging sign came when former Canadian attorney-general Irwin Cotler said that "the Canadian government welcomes this report and is acting upon it", while the UK foreign minister Lord Ahmad said his government "will take this particular report very seriously". If they do not, the number of journalists killed and jailed while doing their jobs is likely to rise. ✖

Rachael Jolley is a contributing editor to Index, and research fellow at the Centre for Freedom of the Media at Sheffield University

50(02):12/14|DOI:10.1177/03064220211033781

Ways of providing refuge for journalists

The top recommendations issued by the International Bar Association Human Rights Institute in their report on providing safe refuge to journalists at risk

1 States should introduce an emergency visa for journalists at risk
2 In the absence of a journalist-specific emergency visa, states should commit to the expedited processing of visa applications received from journalists who are determined to be at risk
3 In the absence of a journalist-specific emergency visa, States should provide an opportunity for journalists at risk making visa applications to provide information on issues of character and security that may arise (as is often done for journalists subject to criminal investigation or charges for their work) and ensure that such visa applications are assessed fairly and accurately in the light of that, and other available, information

4 States should commit to granting visas to immediate family members/dependents of journalists at risk who are granted visas
5 States should issue travel documents to relocated journalists if their home countries move to revoke or cancel their passports
6 States should permit refugee protection visa applications to be made by journalists at risk, from within their home state
7 States should make clear in their domestic law that journalists at risk can fall within the definition of a 'refugee' for the purposes of the Refugee Convention, or otherwise qualify for international protection.

FEATURES

"Disinformation encourages discrimination,
dehumanisation and prejudice against the victims"

NERMA JELACIC ON THE DENIAL OF ASSAD'S WAR CRIMES | SPINNING BOMB P16

PICTURED: The White Helmets search for survivors among the ruins of a building in Amirah, Syria. The building collapsed after an alleged regime air strike in July, 2019

Spinning bomb

NERMA JELACIC argues dangerous revisionists are manipulating free speech defenders

ABOVE:
Nerma Jelacic

THIRTY YEARS SEPARATE the beginnings of conflicts in Bosnia-Herzegovina, where I come from, and Syria, where I work now. Bosnia and Syria are the bookends that encompass the three decades when we lived in a world where our collective conscience, eventually, recognised we had a responsibility to protect the innocent, to bring those responsible for war crimes to justice, and to fight against revisionism and denial. Whereas the Bosnian tragedy of the 1990s marked the (re)birth of these values, the Syrian carnage has all but put an end to them.

Nowhere is this sad fact more apparent than in the expansion of disinformation, revisionism and denial about the crimes perpetrated by the Syrian regime against its own people. As a result, disinformation campaigns have become increasingly vicious, targeting survivors, individuals and organisations working in conflict zones. Coddled by the ever-expanding parachute of academic freedom and freedom of expression, these unrelenting smear campaigns have ruined, endangered and taken lives. They have eroded trust in institutions, democratic processes and the media and sown division in fragmenting democratic societies. Their destabilising effect on democratic principles has already led to incitement to violence. Left unchecked, it can only get worse.

The disinformation movement has brought together a diverse coalition of leftists, communists, racists, ideologues, anti-Semites and fascists. Amplified by social media, their Nietzschean contempt

for facts completes the postmodernist assault on the truth. But more important than the philosophical effect is the fact that disinformation campaigns have been politically weaponised by Russia. Under the flag of freedom of expression, they have become a dangerous tool in information warfare.

I know this, because I am one of their targets.

Earlier this year, the Commission for International Justice and Accountability (CIJA), an NGO of which I am one of the directors, flung itself into the eye of the Syria disinformation storm by exposing the nefarious nature of the Working Group on Syria, Propaganda and Media (WGSPM), an outfit comprising mainly UK academics and bloggers.

The CIJA investigation revealed that, far from being fringe conspiracists, these revisionists, employed by some of the UK's top universities, were collaborating with Russian diplomats in four countries; were willing to co-operate with presumed Russian security agents to advance their agenda and to attack their opponents; were co-ordinating dissemination of disinformation with bloggers, alternative media and Russian state media; appeared to be planning the doxxing of survivors of chemical attacks; and admitted to making up sources and facts when necessary to advance their cause.

The investigation was a step out of my organisation's usual focus. For almost a decade, CIJA has been working (quietly and covertly) inside Syria to collect evidence necessary to establish the responsibility of high-ranking officials for the plethora of crimes that have become a staple of daily news. More than one million pages of documents produced by the Syrian regime and

extremist Islamist groups sit in CIJA's vaults and inform criminal investigations by European and American law enforcement and UN bodies. These documents tell, in the organisers' and perpetrators' own words, a deplorable story of a pre-planned campaign of murder, torture and persecution, a story that started in 2011 when the Syrian regime began its systematic and violent crackdown on protesters.

CIJA's work is pioneering and painfully necessary as it ensures crucial evidence is secured, analysed and properly stored when there is no political will or ability to engage official public bodies to investigate the crimes. Our evidence has been described by international criminal justice experts to be stronger than that available to Allied powers holding the Nazi leadership to account during the Nuremberg trials. This makes us dangerous and this makes us a target – both in the theatre of war and in the war on the truth.

Before long, we were in the crosshairs of apologists for Syrian president Bashar al-Assad and, soon after that, in those of the Russian-sponsored disinformation networks.

Propaganda has been the key ingredient of every war since the beginning of time. But its unrelenting advance in the midst of the Syrian war is unprecedented. The beginnings of its weaponisation can be traced back to 2015 when the wheels of fortune turned for Syria as Russia got militarily involved in the conflict. Assad was on the way to winning on the ground but the battle to own the narrative of the war was only just beginning. In its advance, Moscow's disinformation machinery swept up Western academics, former diplomats, Hollywood stars and punk-rock legends. New outfits and personalities mushroomed, bringing a breath of fresh air to the stale and steady group of woo-woo pedlars and conspiracy theorists from the 1990s.

The WGSPM is one such outfit. Founded in 2017, its most prominent

These revisionists, employed by some of the UK's top universities, were collaborating with Russian diplomats

members are Piers Robinson, formerly of Sheffield University; Paul McKeigue and Tim Hayward, of the University of Edinburgh; David Miller, of the University of Bristol; and Tara McCormack, of the University of Leicester. Apart from their shared interest in proliferating pro-Assad, pro-Russian Syria propaganda, between them these professors cover 9/11 truthism, Skripal poisoning conspiracies, Covid-19 scepticism, anti-Semitism and Bosnian war crimes denial.

The modus operandi of disinformation in Syria is simple and borrows from how it was done in Bosnia: sow seeds of doubt regarding two or three out of myriad atrocities committed by the Syrian regime in order to put a question mark over the whole opus of criminal acts overseen by Assad over the past decade.

IN BOSNIA, ACCORDING to revisionists, Sarajevo massacres were staged or committed by the Bosnian army against its own people, Prijedor

Propaganda has been the key ingredient of every war since the beginning of time

torture-camp footage was faked and the number of Srebrenica genocide victims was inflated. In Syria, according to disinformationists, the Syrian regime's chemical weapon attacks were staged or committed by opposition groups, footage of children and other civilian victims was faked and the number of those who went through the archipelago of torture camps was inflated.

Syria disinformationists make great use of the postmodernist scepticism about evidence and truth in order to advance their theories. They resort to obfuscation, distortion and alternative evidence. The vision is blurred. Questions are important, answers not so much. Context is irrelevant.

There is not much of a change there from the 1990s. The only marked difference is that today's approach to advancing disinformation focuses much

more on tearing down individuals and organisations working in or reporting on the war. In order to make a lie believable, one must discredit those who endeavour to test the truth.

The WGSPM started by disputing that chemical weapons attacks were conducted by the Assad regime, proffering instead pseudoscientific arguments that the attacks either did not happen, or were staged or committed by opposition groups, potentially with the support of Western imperialist governments. They zoned in on two out of more than 300 documented chemical weapons attacks. But two was enough to start sowing the seeds of doubt among wider audiences.

The Organisation for the Prohibition of Chemical Weapons (OPCW) was in the crosshairs as its investigative teams and fact-finding missions returned with findings pointing to the Syrian regime's responsibility for the attacks over and over again. The OPCW was portrayed to be issuing doctored reports in support of the alleged Western imperialist agenda to overthrow the regime, including by the use of military intervention for which chemical weapons attacks would be a pretext. The disinformationists parroted Damascus and Moscow in whose view all of the alleged chemical attacks were staged on the orders of the West.

A special level of vitriol targeted the White Helmets, a Syrian search and rescue organisation whose cameras record the daily toll of Syrian regime and Russian bombs and chemical weapon attacks on innocent people's lives as they rush in to pull the victims out of the rubble. They were branded as actors, jihadists and Western intelligence service agents. They were accused with zero evidence of organ-harvesting. The children they pulled out of the rubble were cast as fake or actors. WGSPM ➔

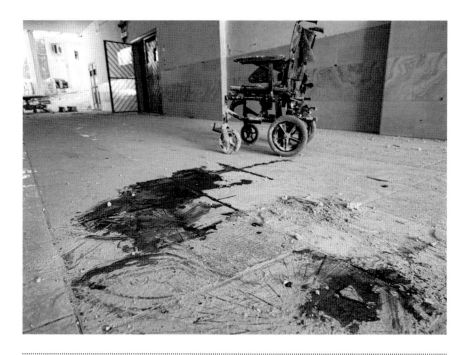

CREDIT: SOPA Images Limited / Alamy

ABOVE: Al-Atareb City Hospital in Aleppo after an attack. An abandoned wheelchair sits on a bloodstained floor following artillery fire in which seven civilians were killed in March 2021

ABOVE: Syrian White Helmets look upon the ruins of a residential block in Idlib destroyed in what were believed to be Russian airstrikes, March 2019.

→ members promulgated theories that the White Helmets killed civilians in gas chambers and then laid them out as apparent victims of fake chemical weapons attacks.

The group's most influential member, Vanessa Beeley, a self-proclaimed journalist residing in Damascus, openly incited and justified the deliberate targeting of the White Helmets, hundreds of whom have died in so-called double and triple-tap airstrikes carried out by the Russian and Syrian air forces. Beeley claimed the White Helmets' alleged connection to jihadists made them a legitimate target. The jihadists connection itself was a "manufactured truth". Beeley has spent years producing blogs and twisting the facts to present the White Helmets as aiders and abetters of the extremist armed groups. This falsehood then proliferated in cyberspace, amplified by alternative and Russian state-sponsored media, and eventually parts of these allegations began to stick with wider audiences.

Last year, a study from Harvard University found that the cluster of accounts attacking the White Helmets on Twitter was 38% larger than the cluster of accounts representing their work in a positive light or defending them from orchestrated info warfare.

Soon, Russian state officials started singling out White Helmets' co-founder James Le Mesurier, branding him as an MI6 agent with connections to terrorist groups. The hounding of this former British soldier was relentless. Le Mesurier was so deeply affected by the relentlessness of the campaign against

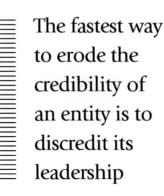

The fastest way to erode the credibility of an entity is to discredit its leadership

the organisation, its people and himself that it contributed to the erosion of his psychological wellbeing and, eventually, his death.

The fastest way to erode the credibility of an entity is to discredit its leadership. This is what the disinformation network tried to do with the White Helmets and Le Mesurier. When they started shifting focus to CIJA, the messaging and the mode of its delivery did not change much.

AT FIRST, CIJA did not pay attention to the attacks. As with the White Helmets, the coverage of CIJA's work by the international media was overwhelmingly positive, although with the difference that we were not as prominent in the public eye. But after the New Yorker published a long read in 2016, within days the alternative media and bloggers produced a dozen articles casting doubt over the authenticity or even the existence of the documents in our archive, branding CIJA the latest multi-million-dollar propaganda stunt.

By 2019, things had got more serious. When The New York Times and CNN within days of each other published articles about CIJA's evidence of Assad's war crimes, inexplicably it was the Russian embassy in the USA that spoke out first, issuing a statement attacking the media for writing about such an "opaque" organisation. Within 10 days, US online outlet The Grayzone published a lengthy hit piece, calling CIJA "the Commission for Imperialist Justice and al-Qaeda", claiming we were collaborating directly with Isis and Jabhat al-Nusra affiliates.

It was reproduced in other alternative media outlets and among social media enthusiasts. But, more worryingly, calls from the people who work in the field of international criminal justice and Syria started coming in. These are not the types who would normally believe in conspiracy theories, and the majority of them are apolitical. However, the more the hit piece circulated, the fewer people focused on its source – a Kremlin-connected online outlet that pushes pro-Russian conspiracy theories and genocide denial – and focused instead on what was being said about the people in their field who are so rarely in the media. Predictably, before long, the allegations raised by the hit piece were being directly or indirectly shared by and referred to on social media by international lawyers and other NGOs in our field. It was a perfect example of the speed and efficiency with which information warfare could penetrate the mainstream.

In 2020, the WGSPM made it known it was turning its attention to CIJA. The focus, replicating that of the White Helmets attack, was on CIJA founder and director Bill Wiley who was perceived by the conspiracists to be a CIA agent in Canadian disguise working with British money and jihadists to subvert the government of Assad and, in the process, enrich himself. It was one year after Le Mesurier's death and, by then, the impact the disinformation campaign had on the last months of his life had been well documented.

* * *

WE WOULD NOT be sitting ducks. CIJA's undercover investigation commenced out of fear for the security of its people and operations. Only three out of 150 of us appear in public. Locations of our people and our archives are kept secret. This is not because we are a covert intelligence front but because the threat is real.

Our investigators have been detained, arrested and abused at the hands of both the regime and extremist armed groups. One has been killed. Among the Syrian regime documents in our possession are those that show that Assad's security intelligence services are looking for our people both inside and outside Syria.

Running investigative teams inside one of the world's most dangerous countries requires a low profile, independence, access and mobility. The nature of the

Only three out of 150 of us appear in public. Locations of our people and our archives are kept secret

narrative falsehoods spread by the likes of the WGSPM was such that it threatened each of those requirements.

Being caught in possession of Syrian regime documents in the country would be a death sentence if our people were stopped, either by the regime or by Islamist extremist groups. Linking the organisation to foreign intelligence services or even to jihadist groups makes them easy targets in the theatre of war that is Syria. Allegations of financial or other types of impropriety are a death sentence to organisations that are donor dependent.

THIS IS WHAT makes these disinformation networks dangerous. By proliferating lies and innuendo and obfuscating the reality about organisations and individuals working in the field, they not only threaten to derail the legitimate work we are doing but also directly endanger the lives of the people doing it. This is not what freedom of expression should be about.

The old saying goes, a lie travels halfway around the world before the truth puts its boots on. The influence of disinformation networks today cannot be compared to those of the 1990s. The proliferation of online media outlets, the growing influence of social media, the increasing embrace of alternative facts and multiple versions of truths have all contributed to the dissemination of a skewed picture of what is really happening in Syria.

Even with the constant reporting by the international media of the atrocities the Syrian regime has bestowed on its own people – with thousands of crimes and survivors' testimonies unrelentingly documented by Syrian and international human rights organisations as well as the UN – Western communities have remained at best on the sidelines in the face of the biggest carnage of this century. The core values of humanity dictate that a collective outcry should have reverberated across the political divide at the sight of gassed children gasping for breath, babies being pulled out of rubble, and emaciated, tortured and decaying bodies strewn around prison courtyards. Yet, by and large, the general population stayed silent. Why? Because the Syrians have been dehumanised on an industrial scale in Western general public opinion.

The purpose of disinformation campaigns is to sow the seed of doubt about what is happening, to stoke fear and ultimately to erode trust in democratic processes and human rights values. And that is precisely the effect of the Syria disinformation campaign.

This has been possible only because the revisionists are no longer a fringe group with limited reach. The trajectory of an untruth about the White Helmets just like that about CIJA is very similar: a blog will come out, which will be picked up by a connection in alternative online media, which will then be amplified by Russian state-linked media, which will then be repackaged by Moscow and presented as legitimate facts worthy of discussion in front of the UN Security Council in New York, at the UN in Geneva, and at OPCW State Parties meetings in The Hague. They have even started penetrating parliaments in London, Berlin and Brussels.

With the help of social media, bots and trolls, and in the era of Trumpian contempt for mainstream media, its trajectory can go only upwards.

CIJA's probe revealed the level of these connections as the Assad   ➜

Reports of massacres are challenged by attacking the journalists who bring them

→ apologist from WGSPM Paul McKeigue outlined them in quite some detail in correspondence with our investigators. The campaigns against the White Helmets, the OPCW and CIJA were not isolated attempts to point to inconsistencies in the "mainstream narrative" of the Syrian war. They were an orchestrated attack on what were deemed to be the biggest obstacles to an attempt to whitewash Assad's crimes.

Although CIJA uncovered the nefarious connections between academics, bloggers and Russian state operatives, the "alternative truth" lives on even when it is proven to be a lie.

For proof, again look at Bosnia. Twenty years ago, Living Marxism magazine went bankrupt after a UK court found that it had defamed ITN and its journalists by claiming the images they recorded in death camps in north-western Bosnia in 1992 were fake. Since then, an international tribunal in The Hague has established beyond reasonable doubt the truth about the macabre crimes that took place in the camps. The journalists' reports were entered into evidence and withstood rigorous challenges offered by the defence in more than a dozen cases. Yet the claim that this was "the picture that fooled the world" and that the camps were mere refugee centres lives on.

My friend Fikret Alić is the man whose emaciated body behind barbed wire was snapped by cameras on that hot August afternoon in 1992. Thirty years later, he is still tortured by a relentless denial campaign. Weeks ago he was ridiculed on Serbian television by journalists and filmmakers who relied on Living Marxism's proven lie to back their claims.

It is a never-ending quagmire. As he told Ed Vulliamy, the Observer journalist who reported from the Bosnian camps in 1992: "When those people said it was all a lie and the picture of me was fake, I broke completely. There was nothing they could give me to get me to sleep."

Living with the nightmare of survival is a lifelong struggle for most. Living with the accusation that what they experienced did not happen condemns them to reliving that torture over and over again.

Mansour Omari, a Syrian journalist who survived a whole year of being bounced around different detention facilities in the Syrian security services' torture grid, recently wrote that "those who callously deny our torture ever happened are torturers in another guise". His words are not a poetic metaphor. The psychological and physical suffering for thousands of Fikrets and Mansours subjected to that denial is very much real.

Yet the survivors are effectively told that those whose denial torments them are doing so in the name of free speech and with the aim of challenging injustices. The idea is preposterous. Disinformation encourages discrimination, dehumanisation and prejudice against the victims.

Instead of being denied the platform from which to inflict further pain and incitement, the revisionists are revered and rewarded with peerages and space to spread the poison in the mainstream.

THE MAINSTREAM MEDIA of today is even more reluctant to challenge revisionism than it was in the 1990s. When ITN decided to sue Living Marxism, the debate it ignited in media circles was not about the heinousness of the lie but about whether it was right for a large media outfit to sue a smaller one.

Today's alternative media go much further than Living Marxism dared to venture. Reports of massacres are challenged by attacking the journalists who bring them. They are claimed to be Western imperialist shills connected to US/UK intelligence services, fabricating reports from Syria with the assistance of Isis or al-Qaeda. But I have yet to see a mainstream media outlet take steps to defend the honour of its journalists, the integrity of its reporting and the truth in the way ITN did so many years ago. The result? Public trust in the media is in steady decline, with a 20% slump recorded in the UK in the past five years alone.

This is not to undermine the journalists who continue seeking to investigate and understand the actors in the Syrian disinformation network space. But they face more of an uphill struggle to get the space for it from their editors than was the case in the past. The question media management should ask themselves is not if it is unseemly for a large media outlet to defend its journalistic track record by challenging the revisionist lies that make it a target of disinformation. The more important question is whether it is right to let such a falsehood go unchallenged. What impact does it all have in the long run on historic record, on the victims, and on journalistic ethics which include seeking the truth?

Academia, too, has been stunned into inaction as a growing number of university staff abuse their credentials to spread propaganda. Whether gathered in coalitions such as the WGSPM, or working as lone wolves, they have become weaponised agitprop agents of Moscow (in the case of the WGSPM and its affiliates, knowingly and wilfully so, as their members have admitted to be co-ordinating with a variety of Russian diplomats to subvert the work of the OPCW, the White Helmets and others such as CIJA).

Universities are hiding behind academic freedom to explain their lack of action to sanction such wholly unscientific behaviour. The professors and

CREDIT: Sofie Gran Aspurvik/Scanpix Norway/PA Images

RIGHT: Syrian White Helmets co-founder James Le Mesurier pictured in 2013

their universities alike claim that these individuals are acting in their private capacity. Yet each one of them links to their university page on the WGSPM website. As plain Paul, Tim, Tara, Piers and David, they would be just another set of fringe conspiracists in the masses. With their full affiliations to prestigious universities listed every time they put their names to a revisionist or disinformationist story, they command credibility.

With media and academia becoming major carriers of disinformation, what kind of a history of Syrian conflict is being written?

The perturbing answer of what awaits Syrians and the future discourse about that conflict can be gleaned from what has transpired in Bosnia in the years since. The denial of Bosnian atrocities has not only seeped into the mainstream but is being rewarded at the highest level. In 2019, Peter Handke, a prominent denier of Srebrenica genocide and supporter of Serb leader Slobodan Milošević, received the Nobel Prize in Literature. In 2020, Claire Fox, who was co-publisher of Living Marxism and continued to deny Bosnia war crimes afterwards, was given a peerage.

What hope is there, then, for the truth about Syria to prevail when Assad apologists are regularly given space in the traditional media, on neo-liberal platforms and within academia? Revisionists such as the WGSPM's Tara McCormack, who lectures at Leicester University and holds a regular slot on Russia Today and Sputnik, frequently appears on the BBC and LBC, too. The DiEM25 movement, a pan-European organisation whose stated aims are to to

"democratise the EU" gives over a whole panel to some of the most vehement Assad apologists, including Aaron Maté who not only denied the survivors their truth but openly mocked them on social media. These are not people who present "diversity" of opinions or ideological or political alignments. Ultimately, these people, instead of being challenged for their lies and the harm they cause to survivors and others, are being given the space to trickle their pseudoscientific revisionism into the mainstream. It is time to stop giving them a platform. And it is time to challenge them with all lawful means.

It might be unpalatable to read such a proposal in a magazine that stands up against censorship. After all, without freedom of expression and academic freedom we might as well bid goodbye to democracy and human rights. But this crucial value is what revisionists clutch at every time they are called out. In turn, such accusations make most of

us uncomfortable to take the necessary steps to tackle a growing problem.

Truth-seeking is supposed to be at the core of universities' existence, but revisionism and denial do not constitute truth-seeking. Academic freedom should allow for robust debate and challenge the conventional wisdom. But it should not allow for incitement of hatred or slandering of victims, survivors, journalists and others.

Truth matters because disinformation destroys lives, as history has taught us. It torments people: from Fikret Alić to Mansour Omari to James Le Mesurier, to countless others whose names we will never learn. Disinformation exposes those such as the White Helmets or CIJA working in conflict situations to additional risk. Labelling journalists as security intelligence or jihadi sympathisers puts a target on their backs. The unrelenting advance of disinformation must be stopped before more harm is done. ✖

Nerma Jelacic works for the Commission for International Justice and Accountability, which gathers war crimes evidence during ongoing conflicts

 What hope is there for the truth about Syria to prevail when Assad apologists are regularly given space in traditional media

50(02):16/23|DOI:10.1177/03064220211033782

Identically bad

With the dictatorship in Belarus detaining and murdering journalists, **HELEN FORTESCUE** talks to photographer **DMITRY BRUSHKO** about his father and their extraordinary 30-year project

ABOVE: President Lukashenko and his son at a rally in 1996

ABOVE: Lukashenko addressing veterans from the Second World War, 2016

"IT'S A FAMILY story," Dmitry Brushko offers. "Two generations, in one family."

He's talking about himself and his father, the late Sergei Brushko. Both men have worked as photojournalists in their native Belarus: Sergei at a time of great upheaval in the country's history – the perestroika and post-perestroika period leading up to the collapse of the USSR; Dmitry documenting seismic changes 30 years on, as the country is seized in the convulsive grip of mass protests and deepening state and police brutality. Our conversation over Zoom naturally revolves around the themes of continuity and discontinuity.

"There are, of course, certain distinctions," said Brushko. "But in principle, [both periods] resemble one another."

The compositions of the images that make up his photographic project, Revision 30, comprising pictures taken by him and his father, attest to this.

He asserts that both epochs are "identically bad", but when he recounts the sorry tale of the attacks on the media site tut.by, where he works, it becomes clear that journalism and journalists are experiencing unprecedented threats in Belarus.

"A week ago there was a round-up at the portal and 15 people were ➔

It's painful to see your colleagues sitting in prison simply because they are doing their jobs – and doing their jobs well

→ arrested," he said. "This sort of thing didn't happen in the '90s."

The editor-in-chief was accused of tax-evasion, a transparent pretext for the state to repress dissenting reporting on the protests that began in Minsk in 2020.

The journalists who were targeted reported on economic, political and social problems within Belarus and went out to protest against president Alexander Lukashenko and his government.

Among them is Katerina Borisevich, who was sentenced to six months in prison for her reporting on the murder of activist Roman Bondarenko. The authorities had tried to portray his death as the outcome of a drunken brawl rather than a politically motivated attack by security forces.

 Most of my co-workers decided to leave Belarus – we don't want to end up in prison

ABOVE: Queuing to file complaints to the Central Election Commission over the refusal to register presidential candidates Viktor Babariko and Valery Tsepkalo Minsk, July 2020

BELOW: Queuing for milk at a shop in Minsk in 1991

ABOVE: Minsk workers rally against a large
increase in food prices, April 1991

BELOW: Veronika Tsepkalo, Svetlana Tihanovskaya
and Maria Kolesnikova who led the campaign in
2020 to unseat President Lukashenko

"Most of my co-workers decided to leave Belarus – we don't want to end up in prison," said Brushko.

He also made the decision to leave as the situation was clearly becoming very dangerous.

When I ask where he is now, he says his lawyers have advised him not to let his whereabouts be known – testament to how the long arm of the Belarusian state has a reach beyond its borders when seeking to quash journalists whose work it sees as problematic.

This is illustrated by the recent detainment and torture of journalist Roman Protasevich, who was hauled off a Ryanair flight to Lithuania which had been diverted to Minsk under the pretext that the plane was subject to a possible terrorist attack.

Even during the period surrounding the collapse of the Soviet Union, journalists weren't arrested, Brushko →

→ tells me. The worst that could happen was getting fired.

He can't say what the future will look like for tut.by. The portal is still live, but his account and those belonging to his co-workers have been blocked.

And yet he remains hopeful that the situation might improve. I ask him how he understands his work as a photojournalist. Is it just a matter of recording events, or can it change a country? At the moment, he sees his main role as informing people to the greatest degree possible about what is going on in the country. He adds that, despite the protests, nothing has actually changed, and without outside involvement, even stabilisation will be

Before people stood for sausages… now they stand for freedom

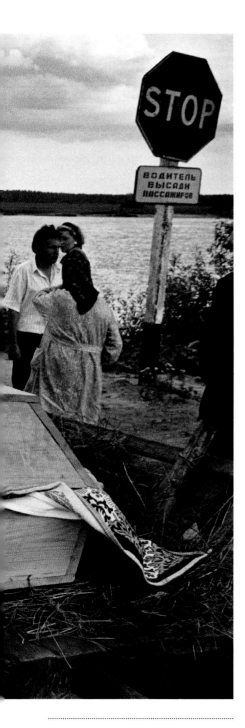

ABOVE: Funeral of a neighbour in the Gomel region in 1997. Much of the nuclear fallout from the Chernobyl disaster was in Belarus

ABOVE: City Crematorium during the Covid-19 pandemic, Minsk 2020

impossible. Changes have, however, occurred in society, and he says, wryly: "Before, people stood for hours for sausages, for food. Now they stand for freedom. Changes have happened."

These photographs, despite their similarities, show that as one historic event ends, another begins.

For the project it was important to think about the tectonic changes that have taken place, he says, adding that he wanted it to be easy for people in any country to understand the differences as well as the similarities.

"Visual language is universal."

A new project will soon take place in printed form in a German magazine based in Stuttgart. Intrigued by the decision to go offline, I tell Brushko it brings to mind the glory days of samizdat distribution throughout the USSR. He sees the influence of printed papers being less prominent nowadays. On one hand he sees the fun in the project, but on the other he sees it as an important way to preserve the role of printed newspapers and highlight a unity between past and future. He hopes

his father would have been proud. We return to the situation in Belarus and how he sees its development.

"We understand that this is a time of change... we will survive it," he said. "But it's painful to see your colleagues sitting in prison simply because they are doing their jobs – and doing their jobs well. The tax evasion stuff is just an excuse. And we shouldn't forget about Roman Protasevich. He worked for a long time as a journalist in Belarus, and what has happened to him is clearly related to his previous work. In Belarus it's a hard time to be a journalist. I hope journalists make it through. Everything should be questioned."

He smiles and spreads his hands.

"And if the authorities don't like it when things are questioned, then we're probably doing our job well." ✖

Helen Fortescue is a researcher at Index

50(02):24/29|DOI:10.1177/03064220211033783

Always looking over our shoulders

HENRY MCDONALD writes about threats made to him and fellow journalists from both sides of the Northern Ireland political divide

WHILE THE DEATH threat was being relayed to me, I was slaloming my way through a human obstacle course in the semi-dark cavernous innards of Madrid-Barajas Airport.

The mobile phone in my breast pocket trilled loudly enough to be heard above a cacophony of destination and arrival announcements. At the end of the moving walkway, I stepped on to the hard floor and took the call that changed my life.

It was from the press office of the Royal Ulster Constabulary (then Northern Ireland's police force), informing me that I had been named in a coded warning to the BBC from pro-British loyalist terror group the Red Hand Defenders. Their communique blamed fellow writer Jim Cusack and me for the death a few days earlier of ex-loyalist prisoner and paramilitary killer Frankie Curry.

The Red Hand Defenders were a cover organisation; they were, in reality, a compound faction comprising the hardline anti-ceasefire Loyalist Volunteer Force and some elements of the Ulster Defence Association (once the largest of the pro-British paramilitary factions), both opposed to the peace process in Northern Ireland.

Their ludicrous accusation was related to stories we had written that highlighted how these two organisations were maintaining the fiction that they were on ceasefire while using the nom de guerre of the Red Hand Defenders to murder and maim. Moreover, we had linked this lethal sectarian alliance to several "no claim, no blame" murders in Northern Ireland during the late-1990s.

Knowing some of the individuals behind this phantom paramilitary force, I realised this warning had to be taken extremely seriously.

Even before I boarded the flight to Heathrow and then another to Belfast,

LEFT: Rioting in April 2021 at the peace wall gate between Catholic and Protestant communities on Lanark Way, Belfast

I rang home. On the advice of an RUC source that I called en route, I told my then wife to take our two-year-old daughter out of our home in south-east Belfast and drive to her parents' house in the north of the city. Of course, I added that before she got into her car she should check underneath it for anything suspicious, and call the police if something concerned her.

Arriving late, bedraggled and on the edge of my nerves, I slept in my parents' house that night and didn't return to my own home until the following morning, when a police patrol turned up at the door. They advised that I should fortify the house in case of attack. Over the next few days I hired a firm which specialised in home security.

Concealed CCTV cameras were erected at the front, back and side of the property; we were able to monitor their pictures from our television. Steel barriers were bolted on to the front door, which was also buttressed against being easily battered in. Panic alarms that fitted into the palm of our hands were left at strategic points around the house and linked to the nearest police station. Sensor lights were installed at the front and the rear, as was a loud air-raid warning klaxon, which blasted out whenever any living thing came too close to the windows or doors. (This caused some problems with our neighbours during the hours of darkness, especially when a fuse blew. Turning the mains switch back on set off a noise that woke the entire street.)

The security measures were paid for by Guardian Media Group, to whom I remain eternally grateful for their quick action and sincere care throughout those times. Cusack's employers, The Irish Times, fitted similar protections around his house in south county Dublin 100 miles from Belfast across the border in the Irish Republic.

All this happened in March 1999, one year after the Good Friday Agreement – the peace accord that was meant to end paramilitary violence on the island of Ireland. →

→ Cusack and I lived like we were under siege in our own homes for at least a decade afterwards, forever watching our backs and eternally vigilant about cars, strangers in the streets or suspicious offers to meet unnamed sources in dubious places. At one stage, the police offered me the opportunity of a personal protection weapon – a gun. I declined, believing that if they were determined to get me then they would, regardless of whether I was armed or not. (Besides, as an opponent of all violence, either state or paramilitary-driven, I loathed the idea of having any firearm in my home.)

We survived this and other future threats. Others were not so fortunate.

Most tragically of all, Martin O'Hagan, a colleague from the Sunday World, was cruelly cut down by an LVF gunman in his hometown of Lurgan in September 2001, murdered in cold blood in front of his wife as they returned from a night out at the pub. His "crime"? He had shone light into the darker corners of loyalist paramilitarism. For two decades, O'Hagan had exposed the main killers in loyalist paramilitary groups responsible for dozens of murders. He knew and understood paramilitary groups intimately having been convicted of running guns for the IRA in early life. He had turned his life around, but his past meant that he was a target for reprisals.

TWENTY-TWO YEARS LATER it is depressing to report that at least one reporter from O'Hagan's newspaper is now living under the shadow of another loyalist paramilitary death threat. Indeed, a number of Sunday World journalists have faced down death threats. One of my oldest friends in Belfast journalism used to joke, darkly, that the official written police warnings informing him that he was under threat were so voluminous that they were Bible-thick.

Patricia Devlin is the latest in a long list of the Northern Irish press/media corps who have been or are in the

gunsights of paramilitary and politico-military organisations. Devlin has courageously highlighted the criminality, brutality and bullying carried out by members of the Ulster Volunteer Force's East Belfast Battalion over the past few years. She has raised the plight of Ian Ogle, a local man who defied the UVF in his area and ended up being savagely murdered. For that and other investigative work, Devlin has been labelled an enemy, and death threats have been made against her and even her newborn child on social media, as well as on the walls of Belfast.

Recalling when the death threats first emerged, Devlin said: "The first threat I received was actually not directed at me but at one of my children, in October 2019. I received a message to my private Facebook account in which the sender threatened to rape my newborn son. It was signed off in the name of neo-Nazi terrorist group Combat-18, which in the past has had links with some loyalist paramilitaries in Northern Ireland.

"Police later confirmed the individual behind this threat was a violent criminal who previously had close links with the UDA. "Prior to this, I had been on the receiving end of relentless social media abuse and an orchestrated smear campaign by individuals linked to East Belfast UVF for my reporting of some of their activities including murder, drug-dealing and extortion."

After Devlin interviewed Ogle's relatives, her personal details including a link to a private Facebook page were reposted on social media, accompanied by dozens of abusive comments.

"I was first informed by police of a threat to my safety in April 2020, when I was visited at home by the Police Service of Northern Ireland and informed of a plan to attack me in my car if I were to re-enter a loyalist area in East Belfast,"

she said. "At the time, I had been writing about attacks and intimidation being carried out by UVF thugs on those living in the area. One of those attacks included a gang of seven masked men who stormed a family home and threatened a mother and her child with hammers."

Devlin was dubbed an "anti-loyalist antagonist" on social media and, according to police intelligence reports, her name was raised at a meeting involving senior UVF members in February 2020.

The National Union of Journalists has said the constant barrage of abuse directed at Devlin is aimed at stopping her and others from carrying out their investigative work.

"I would be lying if I said I did not reconsider staying in journalism. You have these faceless but highly dangerous cowards who are so incensed by what you write that they feel that it's OK to threaten to rape one of the most innocent and vulnerable people in your life. That really unsettled me," she said.

"However, I know the sole aim of those threats is to intimidate and terrorise me out of my job so that the people I try to help don't have a voice. You can't let them win."

The cack-handed, naked intimidation of a third generation of journalists such as Devlin is a direct, unsubtle, menacing form of censorship. It has to be faced down robustly and in a more co-ordinated manner by the authorities. Whilst it is impossible to police the sewers of social media, there are certain practical things that can be done.

We are in a time of political instability within unionism – and particularly within working-class loyalism – following Brexit. There have been suggestions that state aid should be directed at loyalist communities left behind socially, economically and educationally in the

I stepped on to the hard floor and took the call that changed my life

ABOVE: Three journalists killed in on the island of Ireland. Left, Veronica Guerin who was murdered by drug lords in Dublin in 1996. Middle, Martin O'Hagan, gunned down by loyalists in 2001 in Lurgan, County Armagh. Right, Lyra McKee, shot by dissident republicans during a riot in Derry, Northern Ireland in 2019

peace process. Large sums are bandied about, running into millions of pounds as possible inducements to allow loyalist underground "armies" to transform into community – purely political – groupings.

As someone who has co-written two works on Northern Ireland loyalism, I recognise the importance of bringing former paramilitaries into the proverbial big tent. In fact, I have written about groups of ex-loyalist paramilitary prisoners who have created some of the

most dynamic, progressive community projects anywhere in Northern Ireland. They need and deserve state funding as they genuinely attempt to change.

Yet it seems to me that in those areas where threats to the press and media emanate from, the UK government and decision-makers within the devolved Northern Ireland administration should make it clear to paramilitary-linked community groups that money will not be available unless and until all threats to

the media are ended for good. Sanctions or the threat of sanctions should be deployed as a weapon to deter this.

IN NORTHERN IRELAND and across the border in the Irish Republic, there exists another form of intimidation that is far more subtle, better organised and potentially more effective than threats painted on a wall.

As I write, one of the Irish Republic's most tenacious young journalists faces a bombardment of abusive sorties on Twitter as well as barely concealed threats – this time coming from the republican side which believes in a united Ireland.

Throughout April, Philip Ryan broke a series of exclusive stories about →

"The sole aim of those threats is to intimidate and terrorise … you can't let them win"

Meanwhile, that other, far more blatant, boneheaded tendency to threaten and menace reporters never seems to dissipate

→ republican political party Sinn Fein's highly secretive and (some would argue) sinister social media operations. In the Sunday Independent, Ryan revealed that Sinn Fein Facebook pages were being run from outside the country – in one case from an account based in Serbia. More significantly, Ryan later discovered a vast Sinn Fein-controlled mass surveillance system of the country's electorate, known as "Abu" (Gaelic for "Forever").

Abu not only gathers personal information about every voter but also closely monitors their comments on the likes of Facebook to ascertain their projected political preferences. It is an unprecedented combination of "We know you and where you live" and "We think we know who you might vote for". One of its aims is to target not only Sinn Fein's growing electoral base but to urge its cadres within the richest political party on the island to target those it deems waverers for persuasion.

There are now calls in the Irish

parliament for an inquiry into this system. There are questions about whether Abu breaches Irish and EU data protection laws and the privacy rights of citizens. Ryan's exposures of this strange covert system have opened him up to attack by what are commonly known as the Shinnerbots, internet bots which support Sinn (pronounced "Shin") Fein. One tweet sent to Ryan after the Abu disclosures contained a cartoon screengrab from Tom and Jerry with a shotgun pushed through a wall. Another said: "If and when @sinnfeinireland gets into government we are going to have a minute's silence for Philip."

Sinn Fein has consistently condemned threats and abuse towards rival politicians, public figures and journalistson social media. Yet with Ryan there appears to be a sustained campaign to drown out voices like his.

"The social media pile-ons which follow any critical coverage of Sinn Fein are regularly endorsed by Sinn Fein members who like, retweet or engage in the online abuse of journalists," he said.

Ryan believes it is an organised campaign "to bully journalists and others into changing their behaviour". He said: "The majority of the attacks seek to question your professionalism and credibility. The party tries to change the narrative of stories which are critical of Sinn Fein. They turn the story back on the journalist by making spurious claims that they have an agenda."

Meanwhile, that other far more blatant, boneheaded tendency to threaten and menace reporters in the region never seems to fully dissipate.

As recently as April I received a menacing warning on social media from a relative of a deceased loyalist about me linking him to a sectarian atrocity during the Northern Ireland Troubles, even though it happened to be true.

We exist like the characters who survived the outbreak of vampirism in the 1970s TV cult classic Salem's Lot. The survivors roam the planet, on the run, forever watching out for signs that the vampires are coming back. So it is for those writers and broadcasters who will have to watch out for the real-life ghouls for the rest of their lives, too. ✖

Henry McDonald has been a journalist for 35 years and is the author of seven critically acclaimed non-fiction books about Northern Ireland

ABOVE: The journalist Patricia Devlin has been subjected to repeated threats against her and her family

50(02):30/34|DOI:10.1177/03064220211033784

CREDIT: Horst Friedrichs / Alamy Stock Photo

Crossing red lines

Journalists pay the price for clan rivalry in the Kurdistan Region of Iraq, writes **FRÉDERIKE GEERDINK**

THE KURDISTAN REGION has never been safe for journalists. In the last 15 years, at least three reporters have been murdered because of their work and countless journalists have been detained – from a few hours to a few days or weeks. But recently, the region's authorities dragged press freedom to a new low by sentencing three journalists to six years' imprisonment for "spying" – a method to silence journalists that hadn't been used before.

Sherwan Sherwani, Guhdar Zebari and Ayaz Karam were arrested in October last year. At the time, protests were taking place across the region against the dire economic situation and delays to the payment of civil servants' salaries. Initially, the three were not told what they were suspected of, but eventually it turned out they would be prosecuted for breaching security laws.

According to Human Rights Watch, the trials were a travesty of justice, with flawed procedures, weak evidence and a lack of proper access to lawyers. Despite international advocacy by human rights and press freedom groups, their sentences were confirmed in early May.

ABOVE: Camera operator Rebaz Ibrahim films a protest in Sulaymaniyah, Kurdistan Region

In a way, it seems odd that there is this serious lack of press freedom in Kurdistan. The region in the north of Iraq, de-facto autonomous since 1991 – and officially so since the new Iraqi constitution in 2005 – portrays itself to its Western economic and military partners as a haven of stability, progressiveness, democracy and freedom. →

 The trials were a travesty of justice with flawed procedure and weak evidence

ABOVE: Kurdistan, with its female fighters, likes to portray a progressive image

→ Compared with Iraq proper, the Kurdistan Region has a lot going for it. While Iraq was plunged into chaos and violence after the US invasion in 2003 and subsequent occupation, it remained calm: no bombings, no kidnappings, economic growth, elections and power-sharing between the different political factions.

But a closer look reveals a grimmer picture. The region is divided. In the 1990s, after autonomy could be established because of a Western-imposed no-fly zone over Kurdish lands to protect the population against the rage of Saddam Hussein, tensions between the most important political parties led to a three-year civil war. Ever since that ended, in 1997, the southern part of the region has been governed by the Patriotic Union of Kurdistan (PUK), while the northern part is under the control of the Kurdistan Democratic Party (KDP).

THE MEDIA LANDSCAPE and the deteriorating press freedom situation reflects the power struggle between the parties, which are controlled by powerful clans. Although some small independent media remain, they do not form a counterbalance to the partisan media, which are heavily financed by the parties and the businesses affiliated with them. The biggest media organisation is Rudaw, belonging to the KDP. The KDP also influences the smaller K24 network, a Kurdish broadcast news station based in Erbil. The PUK's answer is Kurdsat.

Reaching press freedom is a process. Every generation has to make its contribution, and this is mine

The smaller parties, Gorran (Change) and New Generation Movement, have media as well: KNN and NRT respectively.

As the higher echelons of power are untouchable, the journalists on the ground bear the consequences. KDP media have trouble working in PUK areas while Kurdsat must be careful when it's reporting in Erbil (the capital city) or Duhok, both KDP territory. The NRT's offices in Erbil have been closed several times and have been the targets of arsonists. TV channels are accused of not just covering protests against their rivals but co-organising them, resulting in detentions.

These detentions, says Rebaz Majeed, a journalist based in Sulaymanya, which is in a PUK- controlled area, are something you can try to protect yourself against.

"When I report about a demonstration, I make sure I am surrounded by protesters as much as possible," he said. "They work as a shield against security forces that may want to detain you."

What also protects him is that he works for Voice of America. But ever since the sentencing of three of his colleagues last February, he feels less confident.

"Everybody has contacts in the parties and they will get you out but, apparently, that doesn't always work anymore. Detentions are not just intimidations."

Majeed was another who reported on the protests last year. He tried to take a picture of security forces but they shouted at him: "Move that camera or I will cut your throat!"

Has he been more careful ever since? "No. I work according to the rules of the profession – that's all I can do."

BUT DLOVAN BARWARI asked an uncomfortable question. Barwari is an investigative journalist himself but a lawyer too. One of the journalists who was sentenced, Sherwan Sherwani, was his client in no less than seven earlier trials. He won five of them, while

TV channels are accused of not just covering protests against their rivals but co-organising them, resulting in detentions

Sherwani was fined in the other two. "What do you think", Barwari asked, "when you hear that a journalist is on trial for the eighth time? Don't you think that maybe he wasn't informed enough about his rights?"

Don't misunderstand Barwari: he doesn't intend to blame Sherwani for the injustices against him. He wants to make clear that journalists in the Kurdistan Region are not aware enough of the red lines and often lack professionalism. That is not the mistake of just a few journalists, but part of the bigger picture of the lack of press freedom.

Corruption is a red line. The Kurdistan Region is notorious for it, but writing about it is an absolute no-no. Journalists Kawa Garmyani and Sardasht Osman were murdered for doing just that in 2016 and 2010. Their murders were never solved. They crossed a line by properly investigating corruption and publishing their findings. But other journalists endanger themselves by simply making casual accusations on social media, according to Barwari.

Barwari couldn't defend the journalists this time as he specialises in freedom of expression cases and this one was about security laws, but he has no doubt that his colleagues were prosecuted because of their journalistic work. Judges in Kurdistan are not independent but can still convict people only when there is evidence, Barwari said.

The Human Rights Watch assessment said that the evidence in the cases was flawed, and Barwari said that evidence can be completely fabricated. A defendant can claim evidence was forged, but proving it is something else. It would require an independent forensic lab, for a start. Without being too explicit, Barwari sketches a web in

which journalists get caught and only get more stuck the more they struggle.

That the sentenced journalists were prosecuted under the Iraqi security law is also telling. The Kurdistan Region has its own laws governing journalistic activities which are more liberal than those of Iraq. By prosecuting journalists under Iraqi laws, the Kurdistan authorities ensured they could be punished more harshly.

Barwari would love to set up courses for journalists to educate them about their rights. He set up an initiative with lawyer colleagues, but getting the finances to really make a difference is hard. Even foreign representations in the Kurdistan Region don't support such independent initiatives.

Majeed thinks the Western countries that cooperate with the Kurdistan Region in projects and that support Kurdistan militarily should make that aid conditional on supporting press freedom. He said: "I was once invited by a foreign consulate to speak about press freedom. But I declined the invitation. I don't want to be a photo opportunity; I want them to really do something."

Barwari continues publishing his investigative pieces – about Kurdistan and Iraq – on small websites. He's not politically active on social media. He knows the red lines. His friends sometimes tell him to adopt a pen name to protect his life, but he refuses: "Reaching press freedom is a process. Every generation has to make its contribution, and this is mine." ✘

Fréderike Geerdink is a freelance journalist from the Netherlands who has been reporting about Kurdish issues for more than a decade.

50(02):35/37|DOI:10.1177/03064220211033785

50(02): 38/39|DOI: 10.1177/03064220211033786

Jennings

Our cartoonist considers the parallel universe in which conspiracy theories, such as the idea of a reptilian elite that controls the world, run riot

BEN JENNINGS:
an award-winning
cartoonist for The
Guardian and The
Economist whose
work has been
exhibited around
the world

People first but not the media

ISSA SIKITI DA SILVA says any hope the new leader of the Democratic Republic of Congo Felix Tshisekedi would support media freedom is now over

ABOVE: A supporter of President Tshisekedi brandishing a medal that reads "the people first".

BUILT IN THE late 1950s by the Belgian colonial administration to accommodate 1,500 prisoners, the Makala Central Prison in Kinshasa, the capital of the Democratic Republic of Congo, is thought to house nearly 8,000 inmates, most of whom are emaciated, undernourished, very sick and dying.

For decades, successive dictators – from Mobutu Sese Seko to Joseph Kabila – have been using Makala prison to "re-educate" those who dare to speak out against abuse of power, corruption and nepotism, election rigging and the rising cost of living.

The victims include journalists, opposition politicians, musicians, academics, peaceful protesters and members of civil society organisations.

While some have died because of unsanitary conditions, others have survived to tell the tale of overcrowding, hunger, lack of medical care, sickness, and physical and emotional torture. They also tell of at least 10 inmates who

die every day and who are taken away at night to avoid the public's attention.

"I thought I wouldn't come out alive from the Makala prison. I went through that kind of suffering merely for expressing my views at a public event," said a political activist who spent a lengthy period there after taking part in an anti-government march.

"How do you begin to tell the world that cabinet ministers and state-owned enterprise managers who stole public funds still roam free, but someone who

simply stated his views in the media, in a song or at a public meeting about abuse of power or corruption is incarcerated for months or years without trial?"

If Mobutu trivialised freedom of expression as a white man's myth, the Kabila administration duly buried it, making it a sin that deserved the worst forms of punishment, including detention in undisclosed locations, lengthy jail sentences, torture and death.

The deadly National Intelligence Agency (ANR) had its hands full during the Kabila years, kidnapping and detaining thousands of political prisoners, some for simply stating that politicians were crooks or protesting against Kabila's attempt to seek a third term in office.

The liberation in March 2019 of 700 political prisoners by new president Félix Tshisekedi brought hope and optimism that the country was finally turning one of the darkest pages of

> ## If Mobutu trivialised freedom of expression as a white man's myth, the Kabila administration duly buried it

its 60 years of post-independence by restoring the power or right to express one's opinions without censorship, restraint or legal penalty. But that was not to be. Critics believe that the new leader, who made a "promise to be the one who will promote freedom of the press and sanctify the press as a true fourth estate", appears to be shamelessly following his mentor's footsteps.

His first targets are outspoken journalists and musicians who criticise him, his policies and the ruling party.

On World Press Freedom Day, 3 May, Journalistes en Danger (JED), a local media watchdog, revealed it had already registered 228 cases of press freedom violations under the Tshisekedi administration. These included 47 cases since the beginning of 2021.

Out of these, there were 14 direct or indirect threats, 11 arrests, nine cases of assault or torture and five cases of censorship or obstruction of free movement of information.

Tshivis Tshivuadi, the JED secretary-general, told Index that the current situation was due to the culture of impunity and mediaphobia that has taken hold in the country for years, and which he said would not change without real political will on the part of the new administration.

Banny Mayifuila Kalabanza, a Kinshasa-based journalist, echoed Tshivuadi's sentiments. "Violence against journalists occurs by particular people who abuse their political positions to attack the media but who are never worried about being prosecuted," he said.

Kalabanza said journalists were often victims of one-sided justice. "Any holder of political, economic or military power can give himself 'justice' whenever the discourse of the press does not suit him or her, for example when journalists condemn the rise [in the] cost of living, mismanagement and embezzlement of public money."

Angela Quintal, African programme co-ordinator for the Committee to

The current situation is due to the culture of impunity and mediaphobia that has taken hold in the country for years, which will not change without real political will

Protect Journalists, hailed the courage of journalists in the DRC. She said: "Unfortunately, they have for years worked under threat of arrest and physical violence. Just in the past few months, the CPJ has documented the detention of journalist Pius Romain Rolland Ngoie and security forces threatening radio stations over their reporting on military abuse."

Rolland Ngoie was arrested on 22 December 2020 and transferred two days later to Makala prison, where he spent nearly two months for criminal defamation after an MP's complaint.

"Journalism is not a crime but criminal defamation laws remain a major threat to press freedom in the DRC. This colonial-era legislation is, at its core, incompatible with African and global press freedom norms," Quintal said.

A legal expert who spoke on condition of anonymity for fear of being arrested and tortured by the ANR said the major problem was the corrupt criminal justice system. "There are instances when magistrates, judges and prosecutors get a call from top politicians or businessmen allied to the regime to ensure that a journalist or an academic is arrested and jailed, and the key is thrown away."

Intelligence agents from the ANR were involved in at least 16 of 109 cases of arbitrary arrest and harassment over the past year, according to Human Rights Watch research.

Executive secretary of the Observatoire de la Liberté de la Presse en Afrique (OLPA) Chancelle Nsingi Bamenga told Index on Censorship: "The situation of media freedom in the DRC raised concerns because every

week we register more attacks on journalists. At OLPA, we firmly believe that it is the culture of impunity that is perpetuating this situation."

On the other hand, she said the slowness of the criminal justice system was encouraging impunity. According to Nsingi Bamenga, the way out of this intolerance is for the journalists to operate responsibly, and the government to respect its legal obligations by providing direct and indirect assistance to the media.

She also urged the two chambers of parliament to enact a law on the right of access to information. As freedom of expression continues to deteriorate in this vast, mineral-rich central African nation, self-censorship seems to be gaining momentum.

A musician told Index that he made a painful decision not to go ahead with the recording of the songs he wrote to expose the president's lies about putting the people first.

"Freedom of expression is entrenched in the constitution but, in practice, it has been given to the dogs. I don't want to get arrested just for singing a song that tells it as it is, and sent right away to Makala. It's not a good place," he said.

Quintal said the CPJ would keep encouraging local and international journalists and press freedom advocates to shine a light on abuses. But in the meantime, the situation does not look as though it will improve any time soon. ✖

Issa Sikita da Silva is an award-winning journalist based in West Africa

50(02):40/41|DOI:10.1177/03064220211033787

Controlling the Covid message

The Indian government has been cracking down on criticism of its handling of the pandemic under the cover of "fake news", writes **DANISH RAZA**

N APRIL 2021, Mirza Saaib Bég, a public policy student at the University of Oxford, posted a tweet about the Indian government's inability to tackle Covid's second wave.

Prime minister Narendra Modi's government ordered that the tweet, along with 51 others, be taken down on, based on the premise that it was adding to misinformation.

Bég's tweet had asked about the role of a Hindu religious gathering in escalating the spread of the virus.

Another tweet, by the Indian American Muslim Council (a Washington DC-based advocacy group), which embedded a Vice news article about a Hindu religious ceremony during the second wave was also blocked.

The group responded in a statement: "The government's alacrity in pressuring Twitter to block tweets critical of its handling of the crisis shows the administration's moral compass continues to point in a direction that is shamelessly self-serving."

The government's position is a significant change in rhetoric compared with last year, when members of a Muslim missionary group were labelled as "super-spreaders" – a statement which did not get blocked on social media.

As the pandemic has exposed the country's crumbling healthcare system – India has confirmed more than 350,000 Covid deaths – its government has been busy fixing its image, on both traditional and social media platforms.

The objective of online censorship during the pandemic has been to ensure that a controlled narrative goes out to citizens – one that shows Modi in a positive light.

"This is just a tactic to intimidate people against saying anything even while our loved ones are gasping for life," Bég, who hails from Kashmir, told Index, referring to his censored tweet. "Instead of utilising all available manpower to mitigate this crisis, the government is preoccupied with blocking critical comments on social media."

Facebook, Instagram and YouTube also took down posts that were critical of the government's handling of the crisis, although Facebook restored posts with the hashtag #ResignModi after removing them for a few hours, saying it had blocked the hashtag by mistake and the decision had not been based on the government's order.

The world's largest democracy is the biggest market for WhatsApp and the second biggest market for Facebook.

This is also where social media companies routinely contest censorship attempts by the government.

The latest slugfest is over new rules the government introduced in February.

According to these rules, Twitter and Facebook should comply with the government's take-down requests, share users' information with law enforcement authorities and appoint locals in the roles of chief compliance officers and resident grievance officers. ➔

RIGHT: As the death toll rose, the Indian government fought against criticism of its policies.

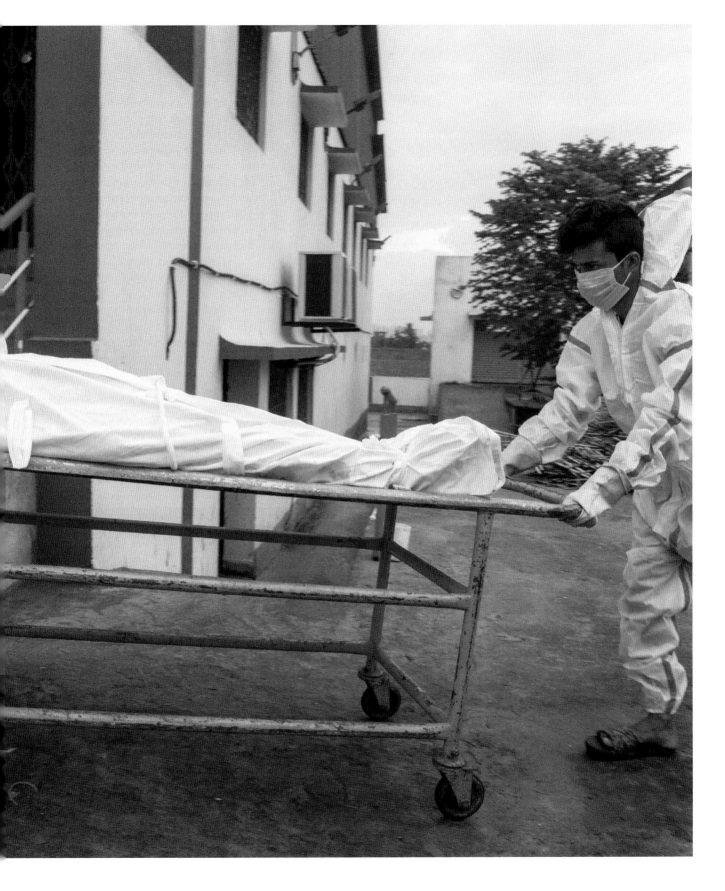

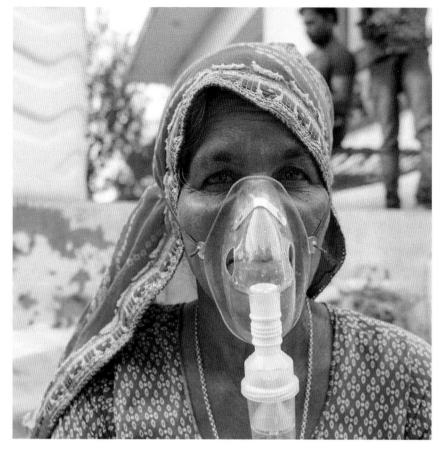

CREDIT: Shimbhu Saini / Alamy Stock Photo

LEFT: An Indian Covid-19 patient wearing a mask.

→ The new rules will also force WhatsApp to hand over information on the "first originator" of messages if asked by the government.

WhatsApp has taken the Indian government to court challenging these rules, arguing that the traceability provision is unconstitutional and against people's fundamental right to privacy as underlined by India's Supreme Court.

Twitter released a statement saying: "To keep our service available, we will strive to comply with applicable law in India. But, just as we do around the world, we will continue to be strictly guided by principles of transparency, a commitment to empowering every voice on the service, and protecting freedom of expression and privacy under the rule of law."

Ten global non-profit organisations including Article 19, Reporters without Border and Human Rights Watch

Journalists die on India's Covid frontline

Reporters have been dying because of Covid-19 as they try to share news of the pandemic, writes SOMAK GHOSHAL

IN THE CITY of Bangalore, often called the Silicon Valley of India, the summer days are bright and sunny, with occasional bursts of rain. But instead of the familiar noise of traffic, an uncanny silence reigns – pierced only by birdcall and the wail of ambulances passing by every hour.

Like many parts of India, the city I live and work in has been in lockdown for nearly two weeks now, desperately trying to curb the spread of the virus. I'm one of the privileged few, with a roof over my head, food on my table and a job I can do from home, while many of my colleagues all over the country are out reporting and risking their lives.

More than 300 journalists have fallen victim to the second wave of the pandemic so far. That's three deaths a day in April and

four a day in May. In Delhi, the city where I spent my formative years as a reporter, I see former colleagues putting out SOS messages on Twitter every day seeking oxygen, hospital beds and essential drugs for their friends and family, complete strangers – and sometimes themselves.

One old colleague, who came down with Covid along with her father and infant son, spent hours every day trying to organise oxygen cylinders for her mother, also a Covid patient who was in critical care for days.

A journalist friend in Kolkata, where I grew up, found herself in a large crowd with no social distancing when she went to get her first dose of the vaccine. As she took a video of the utter chaos and

frightening lack of safety around the hospital, the authorities beat her up and tried to snatch away her phone.

Like millions in India, I am spending my days besieged by helplessness, impotent rage and suffocating anxiety for my family and friends.

Numbers alone cannot convey the nightmare we are living through. Ordinary citizens are gasping for oxygen and dying on the streets in front of hospitals, which face acute shortages of beds.

Crematoriums and burial grounds are so overrun that grieving families have to wait for hours before they can perform the last rites for those they have lost.

In the villages, dire poverty, paltry healthcare facilities and panic have left have written an open letter asking tech companies to defend privacy and ensure free speech by pushing back against government orders that infringe on rights.

Before these rules were brought in, Twitter took a tough stance against the government's takedown requests. Earlier this year, for example, it did not follow the administration's orders to block activists who supported farmers' protests.

New Delhi-based journalist and filmmaker Vinod Kapri took a swing at the government for mishandling the crisis but found his tweet had been taken down.

"Given that the government has increased censorship of mainstream media, [social media] is the last bastion of freedom of expression in the country," Kapri told Index. "It is imperative for these companies to understand their role and potential."

For its part, the government maintains that while it "welcomes criticisms, genuine requests for help as well as suggestions in the collective

The broadness, speed and viciousness with which the Modi regime is strangling critics is something unprecedented

fight against Covid-19, it is necessary to take action against those users who are misusing social media during this grave humanitarian crisis for unethical purposes".

This isn't the social media companies' first brush with censorship in India. The previous regime, led by the Indian National Congress party, introduced changes in the law to stifle online speech.

"There is no government that does not do this," said Pratik Sinha, co-founder of AltNews, India's leading fact-checking website. "But there is absolutely no doubt that [Modi's] BJP has taken this to another level."

One of the tweets taken down belonged to Pieter Federick, a freelance journalist specialising in South Asia. He said that the previous administration

had set a precedent for the authoritarian approach to freedom of expression we see today.

He said: "Many of the examples of censorship under the last regime were one-off incidents. The Modi regime is demonstrating a new, systematic pattern of crushing dissent in all quarters – sometimes even within its own party. The broadness, speed and viciousness with which the Modi regime is strangling critics is something unprecedented." ✖

Danish Raza is a New-Delhi based journalist. He writes on socio-political issues and the interface of society and technology. He tweets @razadanish

50(02):42/45|DOI:10.1177/03064220211033788

millions vulnerable to the virus. Hundreds of bodies are being set afloat in rivers, including the Ganges. These are scenes that generations, including mine – fed on the promises of liberalisation and "India Shining" by subsequent governments – never dreamed of seeing on prime-time television.

In the thick of the catastrophe, another pandemic is being orchestrated by the ruling government of Narendra Modi.

Earlier this month, even as India struggled to keep count of its dead, 300 government officials participated in a digital workshop "to create a positive image of the government". Journalists and media outlets have been urged to spread "positivity" among the masses instead of the panic created by the barrage of bad news.

Perhaps government officials should get out in the field, risking their own lives, and try to spread good vibes among those whose loved ones are dying in their arms for lack of medical care. Or maybe they should stop by those so-called hospitals in rural Uttar Pradesh, India's most populous state, where the toilets are so dirty that even stray dogs don't enter them.

Instead, the firebrand Hindu majoritarian leader who rules over the state charged a man for "spreading panic" when he appealed for oxygen for his grandfather on Twitter.

Yet, in spite of the unremitting horrors of the last couple of months, we are also witnessing tremendous acts of kindness and humanity every day. The youth wing of the Indian National Congress, the main

opposition party to the BJP, is toiling night and day to help the distressed get access to oxygen and food supplies. Hundreds of ordinary citizens are verifying leads on social media for medical help. Non-profit organisations are feeding the poor and homeless and individuals are pouring out their savings to help others.

A shared sense of grief, along with simmering anger, seems to be slowly bringing together people with different political beliefs. There is still fear of the government's reprisal – I feel this, too, as I write this – but every other feeling seems to recede when it comes to the question of life and death. ✖

Somak Ghoshal is a Bangalore-based journalist writing about arts and culture, books, social justice, human rights and LGBTQ lives.

A riveting investigation into a nightmare Orwellian social experiment

"In an expose that is as timely as it is alarming, Geoffrey Cain shows how China is using artificial intelligence and totalitarian repression to turn its westernmost region into a human rights hellhole."

—BLAINE HARDEN,
author of *Escape from Camp 14*

GEOFFREY CAIN

THE PERFECT POLICE STATE

An Undercover Odyssey into China's Terrifying Surveillance Dystopia of the Future

WHISTLEBLOWERS

"It is possible I will never know Reality's true reasons for leaking the document. She will never be allowed to speak about it"

BRITTANY WINNER ON HER SISTER, REALITY (LEFT), WHO LIFTED THE LID ON RUSSIAN HACKING | SPEAKING FOR MY SILENCED SISTER P48

Speaking for my silenced sister

BRITTANY WINNER tells the story of her sister Reality Winner, a US Air Force veteran, who has just been released after being imprisoned for exposing secret papers about Russian interference in the US elections

THIS STORY SHOULD be told by Reality Leigh Winner my sister. I am telling her story because Reality, despite being released from federal prison and in home confinement, is still not allowed to speak to journalists about her case. Reality is being censored and silenced by a government that is afraid of what she might say.

Reality was incarcerated on 3 June 2017. By the time she was released from federal prison in June, she had spent most of the last half of her 20s in prison. For a commended US Air Force veteran with no criminal record, no history of violence, no intent to harm anyone, no plan to financially benefit from a crime and only the best of intentions, every day that she has spent in prison has been a travesty.

As a National Security Agency contractor in 2017, Reality anonymously mailed a classified document detailing a Russian government spear-phishing campaign directed at the voting systems in 21 states around the time of the 2016 US presidential election. She sent the document to a media organisation called The Intercept, which has been known to solicit information from whistleblowers.

Many people ask me why Reality leaked the document. She had everything to lose and nothing to gain. I can speculate that she thought that the American people desperately needed to know that their voting systems were targeted by Russia so that steps could be taken to make the next presidential election more secure.

She helped achieve that goal: the 2020 election was the most secure presidential election in US history.

I can also speculate that Reality wanted to set the record straight about Russian interference in 2016. As the person who knows her best, I can say that she did not intend to harm the USA or undermine national security by leaking the document and, in fact, there is no evidence that the disclosure tipped off Russian hackers to "sources and methods" of US intelligence.

However, it is possible that I will never really know Reality's true reasons or motivations for leaking the document because she is not, and never will be, allowed to speak about it.

Since she was charged with "unlawful retention and transmission of national defence information" under the Espionage Act of 1917, she has not been allowed to talk about the document or even say during her trial why she leaked it. The jury or judge were also not able to know the contents of the document or whether the release of the document actually harmed or exposed the USA. The only two factors pertinent in a trial under the Espionage Act are whether the individual is authorised to share the information and, if not, whether the individual has shared the information with someone who does not possess a relevant security clearance.

Reality was convicted almost certainly because of her alleged confession in the interrogation conducted by armed FBI agents in her home who did not inform her of her rights while a warrant was being served on her home, her car and on her.

As part of a plea deal, she pleaded guilty to a single charge and received a record-breaking 63 months in federal prison followed by three years of supervised release. Her plea deal also broadly prohibits her from future "communication of information relating to classified subject areas" that she had experience in from her time in the Air Force or while employed as an NSA contractor "without first obtaining the express written permission" from the US government.

> Many people ask me why Reality leaked the document. She had everything to lose and nothing to gain

ABOVE: Reality Winner with her six-month-old niece after her release, June 2021.

With a presidential pardon, Reality could live her life without the burden of a felony conviction on her record

ABOVE: Reality Winner in 2018.

The plea paperwork says: "This prohibition includes, but is not limited to, any interviews… papers, books, writings… articles, films, or other productions relating to her or her work as an employee of or contractor for the United States Government."

The language of the plea agreement appears intentionally vague, as though even a casual mention of Russia (which could be construed by the US government as a "classified subject area") by Reality could violate it and send her straight back to federal prison.

Moreover, the exceptionally vague reference "to her or her work" almost seems laughably broad – as if she is no longer allowed to talk about herself or her personal life story. If these stipulations in the plea agreement do not constitute censorship of a US citizen by her government, I do not know what would.

Reality was released from federal prison in June 2021 for good behaviour which is not surprising because she is a good person. However even thought her physical body is no longer behind bars the draconian prohibitions on her speaking to the media continue. Therefore I think that Reality's mind is still stuck in prison and she is far from free.

As someone who pled guilty to a federal crime, Reality is facing more than just the loss of the right to speak freely. She will also have a criminal record that will follow her for the rest of her life, making it more difficult for her to seek gainful employment and enjoy the rights and freedoms that Americans take for granted.

She has also, ironically, lost the right to vote, which is especially harsh considering that she helped protect the votes of her fellow Americans. Reality will continue to suffer the unfair consequences of her brave and selfless actions for the rest of her life without intervention from President Joe Biden

Although we cannot restore the more than four years of her young life Reality Winner spent incarcerated by the time of her release, we can attempt to right this grievous wrong by appealing to President Biden to grant Reality Winner a full pardon.

With a presidential pardon, Reality could live her life without the burden of a felony conviction on her record.

A pardon would also end the continued censorship of Reality Winner following her release and finally allow her to speak out about why she leaked the document exposing the truth about Russia's interference in the 2016 election. The American people deserve to know the brave patriot who stood up for them against her own government.

For President Biden, who appears committed to righting the wrongs of the previous administration, pardoning Reality Winner seems to be the least he should do, considering that Reality's bravery is one of the reasons that Biden was elected as US president in a free and fair US democratic election. We ask the President to carefully consider Reality's case and pardon Reality Winner. ✖

Brittany Winner is a scientist and Reality Winner's older sister

50(02):48/50|DOI:10.1177/03064220211033789

Story of a US whistleblower - a timeline

NOVEMBER 2016: Donald Trump stuns the world by becoming president-elect, beating Democrat Hillary Clinton. In the same month, Reality Winner is honourably discharged from the US Air Force. She later accepts a job at Pluribus International in Georgia, a company sub-contracted by the National Security Agency.

9 MAY 2017: Winner, 25, smuggles a document containing a report about Russia attempting to hack into US election infrastructure through a private software company off the Pluribus premises. On the same day, President Trump fires FBI director James Comey, who was leading a report into Russian interference at the time of his dismissal. Winner then leaks the report to news site The Intercept.

30 MAY 2017: An employee of The Intercept sends a copy of the leaked document for verification, but with key details unredacted. These details, such as a watermark that traces the time and place of the printer used to print out the document, narrow the possible leakers down to six people. Winner is quickly in the frame.

3 JUNE 2017: Winner is arrested and later charged under the 1917 Espionage Act.

8 JUNE 2017: Winner pleads not guilty and is denied bail.

21 JUNE 2018: A request is placed to change the plea to guilty.

23 AUGUST 2018: Winner is sentenced to five years and three months imprisonment. At the time the prosecution declares this is the longest ever sentence in a federal court for the unsanctioned release of government documents to the general public.

24 AUGUST 2018: President Trump tweets "Ex-NSA contractor to spend 63 months in jail over "classified" information. Gee, this is "small potatoes" compared to what Hillary Clinton did!"

FEBRUARY 2020: Reality's lawyers submit a formal commutation request with the US justice department.

APRIL 2020: Judge rejects Winner's petition to be released to home confinement due

ABOVE: Bobby Christine, US attorney for the Southern District of Georgia (front), and J. C. "Chris" Hacker, Special Agent in Charge of FBI Atlanta, left, speak to the media after the sentencing of Reality Winner on 23 August 2018 in Augusta, Georgia

to the Covid-19 pandemic. In July, Winner tested positive for the virus.

20 JANUARY 2021: President Joe Biden takes office and a campaign is launched to ask him to grant a pardon. The campaign is supported by figures such as J William Leonard, the former deputy assistant secretary of defense and comedian and political commentator Samantha Bee

17 MARCH 2021: A documentary United States versus Reality Winner about her case is released

14 JUNE 2021: Winner is freed from prison because of good behaviour. She remains in "home confinement" and is banned from giving public statements. Her lawyer Alison Grinter Allen reveals she is still seeking a pardon.

Feeding the machine

Alexei Navalny is sharing details of his hunger strike and ill-treatment via social media. **MARK FRARY** has been following his progress for Index

ALEXEI NAVALNY, THE Russian opposition leader and critic of president Vladimir Putin is being held in a penal colony. He has been denied medical care, tortured with sleep deprivation and forced to live in unsanitary conditions, with many of his fellow inmates suffering from tuberculosis.

He is also facing new criminal charges, filed since he was imprisoned, and which have been brought – he

believes – in a bid to silence him.

Navalny has been in the colony since February, and we know what is happening to him because of letters which have been smuggled out and posted on Instagram.

His ordeal began in August last year. He collapsed on a flight from Siberia to Moscow, which was diverted to Omsk, where he was treated before being airlifted to Berlin. The doctors there concluded that he had been poisoned

with the nerve agent Novichok, with the Russian secret service, the FSB, in the frame for carrying out the attack.

Navalny spent a month in Berlin recovering before returning to Russia, despite threats that he would be detained.

On his return, he was arrested and put on trial for violating parole conditions associated with an embezzlement case from 2014.

Index and others believe that the charges are politically motivated and designed to stop Navalny from contesting elections. He says he could not register twice a month as stipulated in those conditions because he was in hospital. →

ABOVE: Navalny at an opposition rally in Moscow, 2018.

Here, books are our everything, and if you have to sue for the right to read, I will sue

→ Despite his arguments, he was sentenced to almost three years in a penal colony in Vladimir Oblast, east of Moscow.

It is from there that he is now passing messages to the outside world.

On 31 March, Navalny announced he was going on hunger strike to protest that he was not receiving adequate medical treatment for acute pain in his back and a loss of feeling in his legs, and that he was being deprived of sleep.

"I have the right to call a doctor and get medicine. They don't give me either one or the other. Instead of medical assistance, I am tortured with sleep deprivation (they wake me up eight times a night)," he wrote in one post.

A week later he revealed that there was a high incidence of tuberculosis in the colony, with three out of 15 in his "detachment" showing symptoms.

"Inside there are unsanitary conditions, tuberculosis, a lack of drugs. Looking at the nightmare plates on which they put gruel, I'm generally surprised that there is no Ebola virus here," he wrote.

On the 13th day of his hunger strike, he complained that his books had been confiscated and that others he had requested – including a copy of the Koran he had asked for to better understand Islam – had not been provided.

He wrote: "I came here a month ago and brought a bunch of books. And ordered a bunch of books. But so far, I have not been given a single one. Because all of them 'must be checked for extremism'. It takes three months."

He has now filed a lawsuit against the colony for their failure to provide them.

"Here, books are our everything, and if you have to sue for the right to read, I will sue," he wrote.

Four days later, his captors threatened to force-feed him.

"This morning, a woman colonel stood over me and said, 'Your blood test indicates a serious deterioration in health and risk. If you do not give up on your hunger strike, then we are ready to move on to force-feeding now'. And then she described the delights of force-feeding to me: straitjacket and other joys."

By 20 April, Navalny called himself a "walking skeleton" but revealed that the messages of support from Russia and around the world were sustaining him.

On 23 April, he wrote: "As Alice from Wonderland said, 'Here you have to run to stay put. And to get somewhere, you have to run twice as fast'.

"I ran, tried, fell, went on a hunger strike, but all the same, without your help, I just broke my forehead."

Navalny says that the attention focused on him has meant that he has finally started receiving some medical treatment.

"Two months ago, they smirked at my requests for medical assistance, they did not give any medicines and did not allow them to be transferred," he wrote. "A month ago, they laughed in my face at phrases like, 'Can I find out my diagnosis?' and 'Can I see my own medical record?'"

He has now been examined twice by a council of civilian doctors and has abandoned his hunger strike.

Exiting from a hunger strike is not just a matter of starting to eat again, it must be taken slowly.

"It will take 24 days and they say it is even harder [than the hunger strike itself]. Wish me luck."

On 27 April, he looked back on the previous 12 months, calling it "the year of doctors and nurses and physicians in general".

"I have never talked so much with them in my life," he wrote. "First, the doctors saved me, who was dying from chemical poisoning on the plane.

"Then they rescued me a second time, risking their careers, explaining to my wife and everyone that I should be immediately taken away from the Omsk hospital, where their evil colleagues will kill me (they will not just treat me) on the orders of the Kremlin."

"Then the Charité doctors [in Berlin] turned me from a vegetable back into a human being."

Navalny said in his Instagram message that some doctors had fought a desperate campaign to get him normal treatment.

"Thanks to my prison doctors – I understand that they are just working within the framework that was given to them by their superiors, and therefore by the Kremlin – I can see now that people are sincerely trying to help. Yesterday, the nurse made a mark on my wrist with a pen, so as not to forget the hour when I had to have the next three tablespoons of oatmeal."

He added: "You know, even though what I had been through all these months, I want one of my children to be a doctor. Although the children are probably not already. Well, let one of the grandchildren then."

On 2 May, the day that the Russian Orthodox church celebrates Easter, the following message was posted on Instagram: "Christ is risen. Life and love won. Traditionally, I congratulate everyone on the best holiday: believers (who I am now), unbelievers (who I was), and militant atheists (who I was too). I hug everyone and love everyone."

But the message then took a darker turn: "How long I have been waiting for this Easter? Lent this year turned out to be difficult for me. Unfortunately, I will not be able to share a fully-fledged Easter meal today: I am still in the first half of my fascinating transformation 'from a skeleton barely dragging its feet into just a hungry man'. But I will eat a few spoons of porridge allowed for me with an excellent Easter mood. Indeed, on such a day, I know and remember for sure that everything will be fine."

On 20 May, Navalny said he been craving bread.

"The fact is that I really love bread. If I had to eat one meal for the rest of my life, I would choose bread. Plus, bread is important in prison, you can't eat without it."

Navalny has decide to treat Sundays in prison like holidays to relieve the monotony.

"I didn't take bread all week and on Sunday morning I took a loaf, spread butter on a piece of bread, brewed coffee and had such a divine festive breakfast," he wrote, adding: "The plan almost fell through. They gave bread and butter in the morning, but I didn't have coffee. Fortunately, a neighbour with a jar of instant coffee 'drove' into my cell.

"I opened the window – and to hell with it that there is a grate – brewed coffee, buttered a piece of white bread and sat on the bunk. I took a bite and drank from the mug.

"I tell you: if there were a device that measures happiness, then no oligarch who has breakfast on a yacht, not a single visitor of a Michelin restaurant would have experienced even one-tenth of the complete happiness that I had."

On 25 May, Navalny reported that an investigator visited him in prison to say he was facing three new charges. Navalny styles himself as a criminal mastermind – Professor Navariarty – with the investigator as a Russian Sherlock Holmes.

The investigator alleged that Navalny stole all the donations people sent to the FBK, the anti-corruption foundation that Navalny founded in 2011 to investigate corruption cases among high-ranking

ABOVE: Navalny seen on screen during a hearing through a video link. May, 2021.

Russian government officials.

He was also told that a case had been initiated against him for the "creation of a non-profit organisation that infringes upon the personality and rights of citizens" and for "encouraging citizens to refuse to perform their civic duties". The case relates to Navalny's posting of the film Putin's Palace "without permission".

Finally, he has been accused of insulting Judge Vera Akimova, who presided over the case in which Navalny allegedly "insulted a veteran".

Navalny also used Instagram to send a message to the families of Kremlin critics Dmitry Gudkov and Andrey Pivovarov,

who were both detained in early June on what he called fabricated charges.

"These are honest people who are being persecuted," he wrote. "This disgusting deceitful government is very cowardly. She will continue to eat people one or two at a time to intimidate everyone, but of the people she is terribly afraid.

"But as long as the people themselves are frightened, and are silent, observing the proposed rules, the power will never stop. She will eat and eat: people, families, national wealth, our future."

"They feed on our fear. Don't feed them." ✖

Mark Frary is associate editor at Index

50(02):51/53|DOI:10.1177/03064220211033790

 As long as the people themselves are frightened, and are silent, observing the proposed rules, the power will never stop

An ancient virtue

The right to blow the whistle should be embedded in all societies, argues **IAN FOXLEY**

UNLESS YOU ARE a classical Greek scholar or a student of the French philosopher Michel Foucault, it is unlikely that you will have heard of *parrhesia*. It is an Ancient Greek term meaning "to speak freely". Its use implied not only the freedom to speak without fear but also an obligation to do so for the common good, even at great personal risk to the speaker. In common parlance, it is the virtue at the heart of whistleblowing.

Whistleblowing is not new. In Ancient Greece, Euripedes used it in his play The Bacchae as a medium to remind and instruct the (male) citizens of Athenian society in beneficial social practice. It reappeared in the Roman Empire in the form of *delatores*, and in early mediaeval England under *qui tam* practices, which existed in law until 1951.

It crossed the Atlantic to the USA to be encapsulated in the False Claims Act, otherwise known as the Lincoln Law, which combatted procurement fraud during the American Civil War; and it is the genetic antecedent to the current Public Interest Disclosure Act in the UK, and the Sarbanes-Oxley Act and the Dodd-Frank Act in the USA.

Despite its long ancestral line, there is a basic problem with whistleblowing. It demands a competition of one's loyalties: a fundamental contest between loyalty to values and loyalty to the organisation. Whistleblowing asks the individual to consider between exposing what is

ABOVE: The Ancient Greeks understood the value of being able to speak freely but also recognised the obligation to do so for the common good. The concept is embodied in the word parrhesia, which is being used as the name of a new whistleblowing charity

wrong and an implied debt of allegiance to country, regiment, company, colleagues, friends and even family.

Whistleblowing also requires raw courage; it asks its exponents to place themselves in great danger. Whistleblowing asks that the powerful recognise they need the knowledge that only the vulnerable can give.

In Ancient Athens, the parrhesiastic contract not only offered protection but imposed sanctions against those responsible for the wrongdoing and those responsible for reprisals on the parrhesiastes – the whistleblower. The powerful offered not only freedom to speak openly but also protection for doing so. It is this principle that the Athenians understood

I approach the issue in part from personal experience. I am the whistleblower behind the recent Airbus scandal that started with revealing corruption in government-to-government defence contracts in Saudi Arabia. It has just resulted in a £30million fine for GPT, the UK subsidiary, in addition to being one of the triggers to the deferred prosecution agreements between Airbus Group and the USA, the UK and France, penalties of more than €3.6 billion,

and the removal of most of the group's senior management.

I have found that if we really want to change things for the better then we must find a way to better protect whistleblowers. So I have founded a charity called Parrhesia Inc, which brings together experts in whistleblowing research and policy from around the world in order to focus on the practice, protection and human rights of whistleblowers, by co-ordinating, commissioning and collating research to provide the evidence needed by policymakers to form and reform whistleblowing legislation.

We intend to sow the seeds of the parrhesiastic contract into legislation and all parts of modern society. ✖

Ian Foxley is a retired lieutenant colonel in the British Army and founder of the whistleblowing charity Parrhesia Inc

50(02):54/54|DOI:10.1177/03064220211033791

Truthteller

KAYA GENÇ talks to journalist **FARUK BILDIRICI**, about his new book which reveals how Turkey's most respected newspaper, Hürriyet, became an ally of the Islamists

ON 2 APRIL 2019, hours after it emerged that a government opposition candidate had won Istanbul's mayoral election, the website of Hürriyet devoted its coverage to the false claim that the vote was rigged.

Each of the 15 articles showcased on the newspaper's website that day repeated the unfounded theory that Ekrem İmamoğlu, the Nation Alliance candidate of the Republican People's Party (CHP) and the İYİ Party didn't win. The newspaper refused to report the official tally which showed he had triumphed, albeit with a margin of less than three-tenths of a percentage point (13,700 votes), and ignored statements issued by the opposition.

"The CHP is in panic", one Hürriyet article claimed, repeating a statement by a spokesperson for the rival Justice and Development Party (AKP), which governs nationally. "Interesting development: the CHP has stopped the count," another article warned. "We have identified obvious malpractices," a third piece

LEFT: The book by Faruk Bildirici titled: The Ombudsman of the Media, the Media of the Palace

ABOVE: Faruk Bildirici

said, quoting AKP's municipal leader in Ankara, another city where the governing party lost to the opposition.

Such untruths aren't uncommon from Turkey's government-controlled public broadcasters. But the paper-of-record's choice to devote all its coverage to cancelling the 2019 elections surprised Hürriyet's long-term readers.

Just three weeks earlier, Faruk Bildirici, a veteran Turkish journalist and the last readers' editor, or the ombudsman of Hürriyet, had left the institution that had employed him for 27 years. "I started writing this book shortly after the takeover [by the pro-government Demirören Group]," Bildirici notes in his introduction to The Ombudsman of the Media, the Media of the Palace, a tell-all book that chronicles in remarkable detail the behind-the-scenes story of the transformation of a pillar of Turkish journalism into the most devoted defender of Turkey's current government. "I realised I wouldn't be able to stay there for long. I started collecting belongings from my office and gathering my notes and my archive. As I began to set my experiences, struggles and discussions on paper, I tried to be as objective as possible… and preferred noting down events, leaving the task of interpretation to readers."

The result is a devastating indictment of Turkey's ruling party's tactics of stifling the country's journalism. The 352-page book also solidifies Bildirici's unprecedented role as ombudsman turned whistleblower.

"No, I didn't fear the consequences," Bildirici told Index about his decision to lift the veil behind the country's most powerful media group, owned since 2018 by the Demirören family who are close to the president Recep Tayyip Erdoğan

In preparing his exposé, Bildirici sent all the relevant chapters to figures they mention to allow his subjects to add their own views and correct possible factual mistakes. "Most of the people in the book were friends and executives

I've worked with for many years… Communicating with them helped save the book from being one-sided." He fact-checked all the stories in his book, treating them like newspaper articles written by other reporters. Bildirici even sent a draft to Hürriyet's previous publisher, Aydın Doğan, under whose watch the paper became the "flagship of Turkish journalism" that had rattled governments since the 1990s.

A childhood trauma motivated Bildirici, who is 65, to become a muckraker. In the fifth grade, his teacher allowed him to visit the police headquarters of Gaziantep, his hometown, to interview the police chief for the school paper.

He treated Bildirici and his friends well, offering chocolate and soda. Then a limping man was rushed into his office. "The chief suddenly raised his voice: 'Which leg of yours hurts?' When the roughed-up young man reluctantly showed his right leg, the chief kicked it with all his might. I couldn't believe the sight. I was terrified. The portly man who minutes ago was entertaining us had gone, replaced by a barbarian who could hit a young man… I couldn't take my eyes off the kicked leg."

That day Bildirici promised to become a journalist and "chronicle how people were mistreated" in Turkey.

Bildirici's first office job was at Cumhuriyet, Turkey's oldest newspaper. When he started working at the Ankara bureau in June 1980, the veteran journalist Hasan Cemal (sentenced to →

One day he leaked a cassette to a BBC colleague, an early instance of his enthusiasm for whistleblowing

The newspaper's executives began to intervene, asking the readers' editor to remove parts of his criticisms

→ 18 months in jail in 2018) was one of its top editors. Just three months later, a military coup shook the nation. On the evening of 12 September 1980, Cemal gave Bildirici and his colleagues in the Cumhuriyet office a warning: "Journalists are witnesses of their era. But these are extraordinary times. We won't be able to report on many of the issues. For that reason I advise you to take notes on everything. You can turn them into books later."

Bildirici took Cemal's advice. As General Kenan Evren's rule transformed Turkey and independent journalists came under attack, Bildirici devised ways to make sure stories reached the world.

One day he leaked a cassette to a BBC colleague, an early instance of his enthusiasm for whistleblowing. "Shortly after the coup, when journalists were taken into the Mamak Military Prison, foreign journalists weren't allowed inside," Bildirici writes. "I went there with a modern recorder that operated with a tiny cassette. Before the press briefing, I recorded the footsteps of imprisoned youth who were made to walk in single file. The next day's BBC bulletin opened with that audio recording."

The exposé infuriated Evren's media commissars but Bildirici avoided being found out. In October 1992, he began working for Hürriyet, in whose pages he published a groundbreaking report on a phone-tapping scandal (the subject of his debut book, The Country of Secret Ears, which came out in 1998), and coined the word "telekulak" that describes the practice of tapping the phones of reporters. He excelled at writing profiles of Turkey's public figures and called them "Puzzle Portraits".

Bildirici's journey as readers' editor began on 19 April 2010, after Enis

Berberoğlu, a highly regarded Hürriyet journalist (sentenced to 25 years in prison in 2017) became the paper's editor. Bildirici felt "a new era had begun", happy to see the paper showing self-confidence to face all sorts of institutional critiques. At the time, four titles in the Turkish press employed readers' editors, and the ethics of journalism was becoming an important subject regularly discussed in columns.

Among the problems he flagged early on were product placements and other types of paid advertisements which he considered "a betrayal against journalism". Bildirici strived to make his criticisms constructive, sending his columns to his editor each Sunday morning, often mellowing the language to keep complaints at bay.

But soon after Bildirici's columns appeared, the newspaper's executives began to intervene, asking the Ombudsman to remove parts of his criticisms to avoid angering their subjects.

"I said, 'What are you doing, Faruk? Can you get real results here?' No, I couldn't, because in Turkey the media has these ties to sources of power. But then I reached another conclusion. Maybe it was a struggle I couldn't win but the struggle itself had value.

"So I began a fight I knew I couldn't win… A few months after becoming the ombudsman, I started taking notes of everything. These are the notes I've used in the book."

Bildirici's book encompasses a decade when the Doğan Media Group which owned Hürriyet came under government assault in the form of a $2.5 billion tax fine and pressure to sack its critical columnists. "I couldn't address everything because my main focus was journalistic mistakes,"

CREDIT: John Wreford / Alamy Stock Photo

Bildirici recalled. He compiled readers' complaints into reports and submitted them to editors. Among his successes were changes made to the language used when reporting suicides, but on many other fronts his advice was ignored.

Meanwhile, the ruling party's ire toward his paper had reached boiling point. On 6 September 2015, a ruling party MP encouraged his supporters to raid the newspaper's headquarters. That evening, a group of 200 party members occupied the building, wielding sticks and throwing stones. Bildirici remembers how they "chanted slogans, attacked the security booth at the entrance, and burned the Hürriyet flag… the police merely watched and did nothing". Afterwards the MP mounted a car and addressed his supporters, thanking them for defending the "national will".

was looming and Pamuk told the interviewer he'd vote against the government's plan. The paper refused to publish the interview.

Another interview, conducted with novelist Ahmet Ümit, met a similar fate: 80,000 printed copies of the paper were pulped at the last moment when a pro-government executive noticed the interview's headline, which he calculated might upset the governing party.

In 2018, the pro-government Demirören Group agreed to purchase Hürriyet. The pressures on the company magically disappeared. The bill, about $675 million, would be taken care of by the state-owned Ziraat Bankası in the form of a loan. Bildirici resigned soon after the takeover. In his farewell article, published on 4 March 2019, he wrote: "I've always wanted journalism to triumph. It didn't do so today, but it most certainly will tomorrow."

Bildirici says publishing his tell-all book allowed him to "come to terms with my own shortcomings. Because transparency empowers, not weakens". By exposing the behind-the-scenes events at a long-respected institution, he has performed a public duty.

"I've always believed that journalism is about transparency and that all its machinations should be known by everyone, that everyone has the right to know what we're doing, and knowing about what is happening behind the scenes is a public right." Glad to have kept true to his childhood promise to reveal injustices, Bildirici said: "I did nothing secretly. I'm not an agent. I'm not a cop. I'm a journalist. I've always been open. All my acts strive to meet the standards of journalism." ✖

Two days later, the mob attacked Hürriyet again. This time they brought guns, too. Four shots were heard. "The assailants entered the garden. Using stones and sticks they destroyed the barriers, the cameras, the gates and the windows." The paper's editor ran to the television studio nearby.

"I've been a journalist for 40 years," he told viewers. For the first time I felt my life was in danger."

Bildirici was in Ankara during the raid. "What was more concerning for me was the stance of executives... I'd like to see them openly criticise the attack." The assailants walked free while Hürriyet executives tried to find middle ground with the government. At the end of the same month, one of the paper's star columnists was attacked in front of his apartment in central Istanbul. Four thugs broke his nose and ribs by punching and kicking him.

Terrified by such violence, Hürriyet tried to keep out of the government's way. It didn't work. When the paper interviewed Nobel laureate Orhan Pamuk in February 2017, the editor briefed the reporter "to stay out of politics and restrict the interview to literary subjects", according to Bildirici. A constitutional referendum

Kaya Genç is contributing editor (Turkey) for Index. He is based in Istanbul

50(02):55/57|DOI:10.1177/03064220211033792

Two days later, the mob attacked Hürriyet again. This time they brought guns, too

PICTURED: The
Luanda headquarters
of Angolan state oil
company Sonangol,
which finds itself at
the centre of the
bribery scandal

The price of revealing oil's dirty secrets

Index editor **MARTIN BRIGHT** on the cautionary tale of **JONATHAN TAYLOR**

WHEN JONATHAN TAYLOR approached passport control in Dubrovnik airport last July, he had no idea his life was about to fall apart.

He and his family had taken advantage of the lifting of lockdown in the UK to book a holiday in Croatia and were looking forward to some time together. Taylor, a former oil industry lawyer, had spent eight years battling to expose an international network of bribes paid by his former employer – SBM Offshore, a Dutch company based in Monaco. He needed a break.

But before he had a chance to show his passport, Taylor was pulled aside by police and told he was the subject of an Interpol red notice issued by the Principality of Monaco on suspicion of bribery and corruption (the very crimes he had exposed). Instead of a break, he found himself in a Dubrovnik jail sharing a cell with a suspected drug smuggler and two men accused of violent offences.

The word "Kafkaesque" is overused, but in Taylor's case it is entirely apt. Within days he was granted bail and continued his holiday. But when his

ABOVE: Whistleblower Jonathan Taylor

family returned to the UK, he was obliged to remain in Croatia to fight extradition. He has been there ever since.

In the year Taylor has spent in Croatia, he has lost his job, his marriage has been strained and his mental health has suffered as a result of the isolation. In April, he wrote to the British embassy in Zagreb to say he was worried about his sanity. Staff contacted the local police who turned up at his apartment in the capital, wrestled him to the floor and bundled him into an ambulance. He was taken to a psychiatric hospital where he was strapped to a bed and forcibly injected with a sedative.

He has not been charged with any offence in Monaco, where prosecutors wished to question him about allegations of extortion during an employment dispute with SBM Offshore. After months of legal limbo, the Croatian Supreme Court granted Monaco's extradition request in May, but leaving a final decision on the case to the justice minister. Dramatically, just as this edition of Index went to press, the minister blocked the extradition, allowing Taylor to return home.

Taylor exposed a multimillion-dollar bribery system with its origins in Monaco that stretched to Iraq in the Middle East, Angola and Equatorial Guinea in Africa, and Brazil in South America. His disclosures helped lead to $800 million of fines for SBM →

A network of bribes from Iraq to Equatorial Guinea and Brazil

→ Offshore and triggered the collapse of the Brazilian government. Two former chief executives of SBM have been found guilty of corruption. But Monaco has chosen to pursue the whistleblower.

Commenting on the latest decision on his case, Taylor told Index: "After almost a year in exile, the price of my blowing the whistle has not come cheap, as the destruction of my career and the catastrophic effect on my personal life shows. Monaco decided to pursue me at any cost; they have failed and I am delighted the rule of law has prevailed. I hope the real criminals will now be brought to justice."

The Taylor case has attracted international attention thanks to a coalition of freedom of expression organisations including Whistleblowing International Network, UK whistleblowing organisation Protect, the European Centre for Press and Media Freedom and Index on Censorship. In May, the coalition lobbied the Croatian justice minister Ivan Malenica to put an end to Taylor's exile. A cross-party group of UK MPs also asked foreign secretary Dominic Raab to intervene.

Taylor's lawyer, Toby Cadman, head of Guernica 37 International Justice Chambers, argued consistently that the UK government could and should intervene. "It is not just Jonathan's fate which hung in the balance, it is the very existence of the protections afforded to whistleblowers and investigative journalists the world over."

THE NIGHTMARE FOR Taylor began at the beginning of 2012. The lawyer had been working in Monaco for nearly a decade. His family was well-established in the expat community and his children were growing up bilingual.

His company, SBM Offshore, built and leased floating platforms for the processing and storage of oil after drilling and before transportation to refineries. It was an immensely lucrative specialist business which brought in millions of dollars of contracts. Taylor's

He took the extraordinary step of editing the company's Wikipedia page to reveal how the system of corruption worked

job took him regularly to Rio, Singapore and Houston.

But when Taylor arrived at work on 31 January 2012, everything changed. His boss took him aside and explained the company had received a call from one of America's top compliance lawyers, Martin Weinstein. At the time, Weinstein was working for US oil company Noble Energy, which had been involved in a joint venture with SBM in the west African petro-state of Equatorial Guinea. SBM's head of legal affairs Jay Printz was clearly worried. He explained emails found by Noble on a company laptop indicated vast amounts of money had been paid by an SBM middleman to various officials in the African country, including Gabriel Obiang, the son of Teodoro Obiang, Equatorial Guinea's dictator.

The news was devastating for SBM Offshore. The company was already in trouble after posting a net loss of $440 million in 2011 following $1 billion of charges for overdue projects. For an oil company, to be caught paying bribes is second in seriousness only to a major environmental catastrophe such as an oil spill or a rig fire.

Taylor was asked to investigate the payments and within days realised the company was involved in systematic corruption on an industrial scale. "The business model of SBM was simple,"

Taylor later said. "We got the orders by paying bribes." In the case of Equatorial Guinea, industry and mining minister Gabriel Obiang had been promised $7.3 million – and three top-of-the-range BMWs were thrown in for good measure, too.

Taylor was directed to a safe in the office of a senior executive, where papers revealed the full scale of the bribe system. These showed that a former manager had set himself up as a middleman, doing business for SBM via a company in the British Virgin Islands and taking a 20% cut. A formal investigation, codenamed Project Pandora, was set up: external lawyers and forensic accountants were brought in to find out exactly what had been going on.

A list of "agency fees" paid between 2005 and 2011 was supplied by SBM Offshore's accountants in Switzerland. This flagged up millions of dollars of suspect payments.

The investigation team, which included Taylor, soon uncovered bribes in Iraq, Malaysia, Italy and Brazil as well as the original corruption in Equatorial Guinea. In Angola, a scheme set up by former SBM CEO Didier Keller saw multimillion-dollar payments being paid to a host of executives at state oil company Sonangol.

On 5 April 2012, senior SBM Offshore staff were called to an emergency meeting at Amsterdam's Schiphol airport to discuss Project Pandora. Taylor presented his findings, including a further list of territories dragged into the scandal, such as Greece, India, Nigeria and Vietnam. He recommended informing the authorities in all affected territories.

For 10 hours the company thrashed out its options, but in the end decided on a policy of "containment" – limited disclosure coupled with a cover-up of the full scale of the fraud.

What the company did not know was that Taylor had already informed the US Securities and Exchange Commission, which investigates corporate fraud, via his American lawyer. Nor did his bosses realise he was recording every meeting.

Within six months, Taylor was gone. After failing to persuade his bosses to report the corruption scandal, he parted company with SBM in June 2012.

IT TOOK NEARLY 18 months for Taylor to go public on his claims. Initially gagged by the conditions of the termination agreement he had signed with SBM Offshore, he was worried that he would never work in the oil business again. He also tried during this period to renegotiate the terms of his contract, something he would later come to regret.

Eventually he took the extraordinary step of editing the company's Wikipedia page to reveal how the system of corruption worked. The evidence was damning. In April 2014, he began co-operating with the Dutch authorities.

In November 2014, SBM paid $240 million to Dutch prosecutors in an out-of-court settlement. As part of the deal, it admitted to the corruption of public officials, mainly in Angola, Brazil and Equatorial Guinea, between 2007 and 2011. A similar arrangement, a deferred prosecution agreement, was reached in the USA in 2017. In the UK, the company admitted to corrupt payments stretching back more than 20 years. Tony Mace, the British CEO of SBM at the time, received a three-year prison sentence for fraud.

In March this year, Didier Keller – Mace's predecessor and the man responsible for setting up the bribery system – was finally brought to justice in Switzerland, where he was found guilty of paying $6.8 million of bribes into bank accounts controlled by senior Sonangol figures. The Swiss prosecutor explained that any contract won by SBM Offshore had to be approved at various levels in the Sonangol hierarchy, where certain officials had the power of veto. At the very top of the pyramid was chief executive Manuel Vicente, who went on to serve as Angola's vice-president.

Writing about the oil giant in his Angolan travelogue Blue Dahlia, Black Gold, Daniel Metcalfe explained that "Sonangol is the company every Angolan dreams of working for... it is the only company in Angola that really matters". It accounts for 90% of the country's export revenues – about $33 billion – with sidelines in hotels, banks and real estate. Its headquarters, which dominate the central square of Luanda, cost $131 million and is shaped, naturally, like an oil rig.

Because it so comprehensively dominates the Angolan economy, other sectors struggle to thrive. And the corruption of Angolan officials has become notorious. The country currently lies 146th out of 198 in the Transparency International corruption index, ranking the same as Bangladesh and Guatemala and just below Iran.

Little of Angola's oil wealth trickles down to its people, with 40% of Angolans living in poverty, a figure that rises in rural areas which the wealth does not touch.

A RECKONING OF sorts is coming in Angola. In 2017, president Jose Eduardo dos Santos stepped down after 38 years in power in favour of his chosen successor, João Lourenço. However, Lourenço – known as "J-Lo" – proved to be no pushover and began dismantling the vast business empire constructed by the dos Santos family.

In 2020, $1 billion of assets belonging to Isabel dos Santos, the daughter of the former dictator, were frozen and her half-brother, Jose

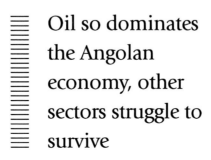

Oil so dominates the Angolan economy, other sectors struggle to survive

Filomeno dos Santos, received a five-year prison sentence for corruption. Former president dos Santos and his deputy Vicente – sometimes described as Africa's richest man – are protected by an immunity agreement put in place after they left office.

Until now, the major oil companies have been largely untouched by the SBM Offshore scandal and Angolan corruption. But a year ago, Taylor began working with Ken Hurwitz, a senior anti-corruption lawyer at the Open Society Justice Initiative based in New York. Hurwitz was building a case against various Sonangol officials to deliver to the authorities in Portugal, where Vicente was accused of bribing a judge. He came across the name of an obscure company whose shareholders included various close associates of Vicente. When Taylor looked into the Angolan company, he discovered documents that showed it had been at the centre of a deal struck between SBM Offshore, Sonangol and America's largest oil company Exxon-Mobil. Taylor has also discovered details of SBM's links with BP in Angola.

The SBM Offshore corruption scandal is a truly global story. It has now led to inquiries in the Netherlands, Switzerland and Brazil as well as the UK and the USA. The $800 million of fines paid by SBM were intended to draw a line under the affair. But that depended on the disclosure of the full scale of the corruption. If the authorities were not told about other deals, it is possible that those agreements will unravel.

It would suit Monaco, SBM Offshore, "big oil" and various kleptocrat elites in Africa if Taylor were to be silenced, which is precisely why campaigners have been so committed to his cause and to bringing those responsible for the corruption to justice. ✖

Martin Bright is editor of Index on Censorship magazine

50(02):58/61|DOI:10.1177/03064220211033795

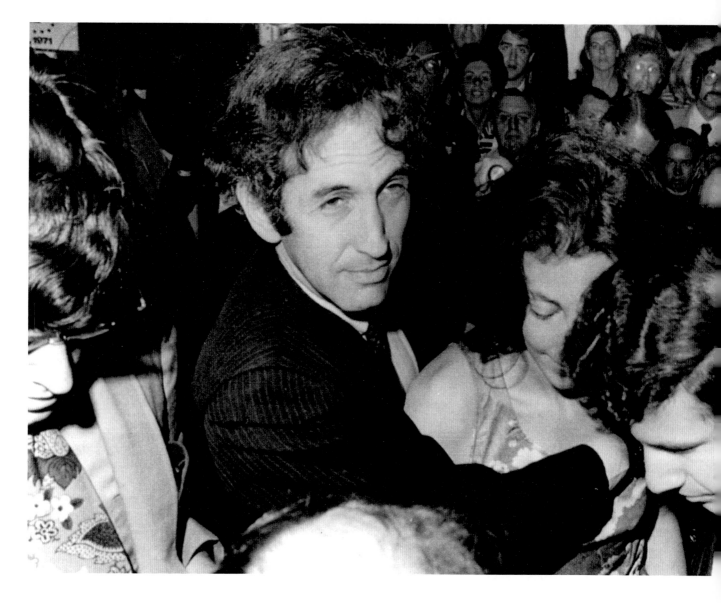

The original whistleblower

MARK FRARY talks to **DANIEL ELLSBERG** about the importance of leaks

CREDIT: Everett Collection Historical / Alamy Stock Photo

WHISTLEBLOWER DANIEL ELLSBERG, whose leaks 50 years ago this summer aimed the spotlight at the US government's secret escalation of the conflict in Vietnam over the course of five presidential administrations, is clear that such shattering revelations should not happen just once in a generation.

"There should be something of the order of the Pentagon Papers once a year if not more often," he said.

Ellsberg speaks to me over Zoom from his home in California's Bay Area shortly after celebrating his 90th birthday. His mind is as sharp as ever and his belief that government wrongdoing should be uncovered is as strong as it was more

than five decades ago. His leaking of thousands of pages of critical failings of presidents from John F Kennedy through to Richard Nixon in US involvement in Vietnam – the Pentagon Papers – proved damning, and ultimately led to Tricky Dicky's impeachment.

Instead of such yearly disclosures of wrongfully withheld information,

ABOVE: Pentagon Papers whistleblower Daniel Ellsberg with his wife Patricia as he surrenders to the authorities in Boston in 1971.

Ellsberg says it took 39 years before there was a leak of a similar scale – Chelsea Manning's disclosure of hundreds of thousands of US diplomatic cables and their subsequent publication by Julian Assange on Wikileaks in 2010.

Ellsberg is of the belief that the world needs a new generation of whistleblowers to keep his government in check.

"US foreign policy is largely conducted as a covert, plausibly denied, imperial policy," he said. "We deny we are an empire, and we deny the means we use, the means which every empire uses to maintain its hegemony – torture, paramilitary invasion, assassination. This is the standard for everybody who seeks a global influence over countries and gets involved in regime change the way we do."

But a career as a whistleblower is unlikely to be recommended to young people emerging from education any time soon.

"I have never heard of anyone wanting to be a whistleblower," said Ellsberg. "People admire it when they see it, but it is a strange career to set out on – and it's not a career because you generally only get to do it once. Employers believe you won't tell their dirty secrets no matter how criminal, illegal, wrongful or dangerous your bosses may be."

He says that people entering the world of work for the first time need to understand what they are signing up for.

"When young people sign agreements [with their employers] under which they will be asked to not reveal any secrets they become privy to in their job they should take into account that they don't really have a right to keep that promise in all circumstances," he said. "Circumstances may well arise where it is wrong to keep silent about information that has come to your attention because other lives are at stake, or perhaps the constitution is being violated and it is wrongful to keep that promise.

"It doesn't occur to you that you could be asked to take part in very wrongful or criminal activities. In your eyes you are not joining the Mafia, yet you make a promise of secrecy like the Mafia without knowing what you are going to be asked to do. This is why you should have your fingers crossed when you make that promise."

Ellsberg relates being invited to a meeting in Stockholm to give an award to Ingvar Bratt, who had exposed illegal sales by arms dealer Bofors.

There should be something of the order of the Pentagon Papers once a year if not more often

"Bratt told me that he was explaining to his young son – who was 10 or so – that he was meeting me and explained what I had done. He said to his son: 'Wasn't that a good thing to do?' His son said very soberly: 'Oh no. He shouldn't have done that; you should never break a promise'. That is how we are all brought up.

"Young people should remain open to the idea that you may be called on to risk your job, your career, your relationships with other people by telling the truth even if you have promised not to do that. It is very unusual advice for young people to hear; it will not improve their career prospects, but it will possibly save a lot of lives."

Ellsberg is in regular contact with other whistleblowers – a club with a very exclusive membership.

"Whistleblowers believe themselves to be quite ordinary," he said. "They don't think that what they did is particularly unusual. They think what they did was the thing anyone would have done in the circumstances.

"But stepping back from their views, it is very unusual for people to do what they did in those circumstances. In almost every case their colleagues knew what was happening and that [the wrongdoing] should be known, but they did not ask themselves if they should be the one to tell.

"There is something unfortunately quite rare about whistleblowing, and that is not good for the future of our species. It means that when terribly →

LEFT: Daniel Ellsberg with fellow whistleblower Thomas Drake (left), who revealed details of surveillance by the US National Security Agency in 2015. The lawyer Jesselyn Radack is also pictured.

→ dangerous processes are at work, like wrongful wars or the climate crisis, we can't count on people to step forward and tell us what we need to know.

"Very few people get beyond the point of saying 'This should be known' to the point of saying 'No one else is going to do it, so I have to do it'. That turns out to be an almost unpredictable reaction. It is a matter of personal responsibility and moral courage."

Moral courage is a vital attribute of a whistleblower, since being ostracised is a frequent outcome.

"People will do almost anything and go along with anything rather than be expelled from a group that they value.," said Ellsberg.

But being cast out is often the least of the worries of would-be whistleblowers, as the act comes with significant costs.

"Chelsea Manning said she was willing to face life in prison or even death," said Ellsberg. "[Edward] Snowden said at one point there were things worth dying for and he hadn't been killed for it yet, but he was at considerable risk of that – and it could still happen.

"The government does everything it can to magnify those costs both for

the whistleblower and anyone who might want to imitate her or him. There is the stigma of being called crazy, being called criminal. The government really goes into trying to defame the whistleblower in different ways, and often quite successfully.

"Assange and Snowden have been made into real pariahs. I was called a lot of names at the time and if you are not willing to be called names that are painful but inappropriate and unearned then this is not something you should go into."

Being a whistleblower today is different from how it was 50 years ago. Technology has made it easier to share information but has also made leaks easier to trace.

"Reality Winner's case is a classic example of the technical possibility of tracing the source. They were able

to see who had probably released it. It illustrates that it is easy to get the information out, but it is relatively hard to hide the fact that you were the one who was the source.

Ellsberg says Winner, who leaked classified information about Russian involvement in the 2016 US presidential election, "did what she should have done".

Should she have been sent to prison? "Absolutely not."

"There was evidence of Russian involvement [in the election] which the administration was denying. It was important for the public to know that," he said.

Winner has now been released from prison early thanks to good behaviour (see page 48) but is still prevented from speaking about the case.

Ellsberg believes a pardon for Winner from president Joe Biden looks unlikely, especially as he has not done the same for Julian Assange.

"Biden, or someone under him who was a holdover from the Trump administration, has renewed the appeal to extradite Julian Assange and that is not entirely surprising. Biden called Assange a 'hi-tech terrorist' at the time of the releases that he is indicted for in 2010," he said.

"It goes against the fact that the Obama administration declined to indict Assange on the very good conclusion [that he was] a journalist releasing information to the American public.

Whistleblowers believe themselves to be quite ordinary. They think what they did was the thing anyone would have done in the circumstances

Daniel Ellsberg and the Pentagon Papers

DANIEL ELLSBERG WAS born in Chicago in 1931. After graduating from Harvard in 1952 with a BA summa cum laude in economics, he studied for a year on a Woodrow Wilson Fellowship at King's College, Cambridge.

From 1954 to 1957 he served in the US Marine Corps and in 1962 he earned his PhD in economics at Harvard.

Ellsberg joined the Rand Corporation – a policy thinktank offering research and advice to the US armed forces - in 1959 as a strategic analyst. As part of this role he acted as a consultant to the White House and US Defence Department, specialising in problems of the command and control of nuclear weapons and drafting the operational plans for general nuclear war.

In the mid-1960s, he joined the Defence Department for a year as special assistant to assistant secretary of defence John McNaughton, working on the escalation of the war in Vietnam before serving two years with the US State Department in Saigon.

He returned to the Rand Corporation in 1967 where he worked on the top-secret McNamara study, looking at US decision-making in Vietnam between 1945 and 1968.

Ellsberg says the material that became known globally as the Pentagon Papers did not at first appear to be anything special.

"They didn't look that effective as they ended in 1968. I assumed that the president [Richard Nixon] would say 'This is old history and doesn't have anything to do with me'. It was just a fifth president following in the footsteps of four previous presidents," said Ellsberg.

The 7,000-page report was duplicated on a Xerox photocopier with the help of his Rand colleague Anthony J Russo.

"In those days it was a fairly slow process, copying just one page at a time," he said. "Keeping it secret wasn't a problem. In those days, the guards at the Rand Corporation who checked everyone in and out didn't get to check in your briefcase. It made my heart pound when I went past them the first few times with a briefcase full of top-secret documents."

If 7,000 pages were not enough, he also copied thousands more pages of documents relating to US nuclear policy, which he revealed in his book The Doomsday Machine, published in 2017.

The decision to leak came after listening to anti-Vietnam War activist Randy Kehler.

"It was seeing someone with whom I could identify who had a career and who was willing to go to prison," he said. "It made me ask myself 'What can I do now that I am ready to go to prison?'"

Ellsberg leaked the report in 1971 to The New York Times, The Washington Post and 17 other newspapers but it was the Times which took the plunge after sitting on the explosive material for months. On Sunday 13 June 1971, it published its first excerpts from the report, but its wider circulation was held up for 15 days due to a court order requested by the Nixon administration.

The release of information showed that the USA had illegally expanded the scope of the Vietnam War and that the administration of president Lyndon Johnson had lied to the public and Congress.

In early 1973, Ellsberg surrendered to the authorities and faced eight charges of espionage, six of theft and one of conspiracy which, if convicted, carried a possible sentence of 115 years.

In the event, Ellsberg did not go to jail for even a single year.

After a four-and-a-half month trial, the charges against him were dropped after the presiding judge, William Matthew Byrne Jr, ordered a mistrial over "improper government conduct" in relation to illegal evidence-gathering.

It was revealed during the trial that representatives of the administration had illegally broken into the office of Ellsberg's psychiatrist and attempted to steal files in order to discredit him. The FBI had also set up illegal wiretaps on the home phone of security consultant Morton Halperin, through which the FBI overheard his conversations with Ellsberg about the papers.

Indirectly, the Pentagon Papers would lead to Nixon's impeachment. His anger at constant leaks led to the illicit wiretapping and burglaries that ended with his downfall over the Watergate scandal.

Biden could have gone along with that. I still have some small hope that he will [pardon him] as he should, but I don't count on it."

Ellsberg is convinced that Assange deserves protection for leaking the Manning cables.

"He certainly acted as a journalist, as a publisher specifically – as much as any of the publishers with whom he shared the Chelsea Manning documents. [Assange's] philosophy of journalists is actually broader than some others and reflects a relatively new digital age philosophy which I don't entirely share. He believes in almost absolute transparency with the government, but not of private people. Although I think there are secrets that I am in favour of not releasing, that's not true of the material he is indicted for in 2010."

I ask Ellsberg whether he would do the same today as he did 50 years ago and he says he wouldn't be happy sitting around for months waiting for a paper to dare to publish.

"I would still go first to The New York Times, but If I didn't hear from them I would go elsewhere. If I felt that the Times was holding back, as it seemed to be doing for several months when I was dealing with [then NYT reporter] Neil Sheehan, I would have to have gone to another channel such as Wikileaks or the web directly. Of course, that didn't exist then."

He says "the chance of being fingered is greater than it was before", but concurs that he would do it again.

In one sense, he already has, with the publication of The Doomsday Project on US nuclear policy in 2017 that was based on further material he had copied in his time at government- funded military research organisation Rand Corporation in the 1960s.

That makes Ellsberg that very rare thing: a career whistleblower. ✖

Mark Frary is associate editor at Index

50(02):62/65|DOI:10.1177/03064220211033796

Fishrot, the global stench of scandal

RAINER WINTERS writes about Jóhannes Stefánsson who exposed widespread corruption at the heart of the global fishing industry

HE WAS JUST an Icelandic fisherman, but his life changed overnight when he went into global fishing management. What Jóhannes Stefánsson discovered would blow the whole industry apart.

In what became known as the Fishrot scandal, Stefansson exposed what was happening in the multi-billion dollar fishing and fish-processing business, including bribery, tax evasion and the plundering of massive fish stocks which belonged to the people of Namibia.

For his trouble, he would be harassed and his life would be threatened.

His efforts have now been internationally recognised, On 9 March 2021, he won the WIN WIN Gothenburg Sustainability Award, given this year to recognise anti-corruption initiatives which are crucial for sustainable development throughout the world.

I met Stefánsson last year via LinkedIn. We had many interests in common: I've supported whistleblowers for years, and at university I did some work on the subject of over-fishing.

ABOVE: Whistleblower Jóhannes Stefánsson (left) pictured working for Samherji in 2012

What Stefánsson told me was shocking. While he was employed by the Icelandic fishing and fish processing giant Samherji, he discovered a huge international network of corruption and money laundering connected with his former employer. He told me he had probably been poisoned because of that controversy.

He told me he had become a key witness in corruption cases and was in constant danger. Stefánsson believes all kinds of different forces want to silence him. So far, they haven't succeeded. The harder they fight against him, the more solidarity he gets even in his home of Iceland. According to a survey from early 2021 more than 92% of all Icelanders believe that his employers, Samherji bribed politicians in Namibia.

Up in the cold North Atlantic, hardly any crops grow, and fishing in Iceland is (almost) everything. But as the fishing grounds in Europe have become overfished, this small country's large trawlers are now going to regions thousands of kilometres away. The waters off the coasts of West Africa where billions of fish thrive are happy hunting grounds for their international fishing fleets and the coastal waters off Namibia particularly so. Here mackerel, sardines, tuna and hake are caught and sold to supermarkets across the world including in the UK to Tesco, Marks and Spencer and Sainsbury's.

In 2007, Stefánsson who came from a family of fishermen, started working for Katla Seafood, a subsidiary of Samherji.

At first the company was working in Morocco, but when Iceland found

ABOVE: The former Samherji ship Heinaste after a large haul.

itself shut out of the market by EU deals, Samherji turned to Namibia with its rich fishing grounds where Stefánsson was sent to buy fishing quotas.

In November 2011, Stefánsson had his first glimpse of how deals worked when he, along with his boss Aðalsteinn Helgasson, received an offer of cheap fishing quotas.

Two negotiators invited Samherji executives to a secret meeting on the farm of fishing minister Bernhard Esau,

CREDIT: Photos from Fishrot files

now in custody on corruption charges, in order to discuss the quota deals. The Icelanders could receive cheaper quotas and the difference from the normal price could be paid through discreet channels.

In the end, the funds were supposed to make their way to the governing party, SWAPO. Namibia is seeking to extradite Icelandic executives from Samherji as part of their investigation

into bribery allegations worth $200 million (or $3 billion Namibian dollars).

According to Stefánsson, in 10 years Samherji made a profit of $660 million. Samherji fishes about 20% of its worldwide catch in Namibia. It runs 40 ships, five fish farms and 13 land-based factories. The investments are huge.

Much of the communication between the company directors and officials in

Namibia passed through Stefánsson, who was acting as the representative of other subsidiaries, including Katla Seafood Namibia and Arcticnam Fishing.

To avoid taxation, Samherji also constructed an enormous company network in which assets were moved back and forth in such a way that as little tax as possible was paid and money laundering and bribes could be hidden away.

The money was presumed laundered through Mauritius, Cyprus and the Marshall Islands. In Cyprus alone, the company has various subsidiaries – all in the same office. →

 ## The waters of West Africa are happy hunting grounds for Icelandic fleets

ABOVE: Members of the team working at the Namibia financial intelligence centre

→ Thousands of documents showed the transactions in detail. In 2016, when the business practices got too much for him, Stefánsson left the company, taking more than 30,000 documents, memos and pictures with him on a memory stick. He delivered those documents to Namibia's Financial Intelligence Centre which works independently from government. They immediately saw organised crime at work and have been tenacious in pursuing both Nambians and Icelanders. Stefánsson is their star witness. It turned out 27 countries were involved, meaning 27 jurisdictions for money laundering and tax evasion. In 2019, WikiLeaks published the first documents. Al Jazeera received them

and sent undercover journalists to Africa, some of whom filmed ministers with hidden cameras. The scandal was dubbed "Fishrot".

Al Jazeera's documentary was political dynamite in Namibia. Broadcast just before the elections, it led to the all-powerful SWAPO suffering severe setbacks in the presidential and national assembly for the first time in 30 years.

Later, in the regional government and city council elections, SWAPO also lost its usual majorities to opposition parties in many constituencies. Samherji seeing its business dealing exposed, hit back. When Stefánsson's health deteriorated, his former employer depicted him as unreliable, an alcoholic and a drug addict. When the Norwegian Financial Supervisory Authority imposed a money laundering fine of €40 million on Samherji's business bank, DNB ASA, Samherji announced that the penalty had nothing to do with it, this despite the fact the bank accepted the punishment, and the FSA stressed that the fine related principally to Samherji.

The company also went after those who reported the case, including employees of Iceland state broadcaster RÚV. Samherji lodged a complaint with the Ethics Commission in Iceland over social media content. In Namibia,

Samherji was accused by the Namibian Journalists Association of harassing journalists and the association issued an international appeal for Samherji to stop.

In 2019, Icelandic politicians became involved and started to defend Samherji. Foreign minister Gunnar Bragi Sveinsson accused the newspaper Stundin, and also RÚV, of practising tabloid journalism.

Samherji went on the offensive too, telling German daily Süddeutsche Zeitung that Stefánsson was on "a personal revenge campaign". In London, mysterious people, connected in all likelihood to Namibian politics, started shadowed Stefánsson and the bodyguard he has been forced to hire.

For Stefánsson, Fishrot continues to reverberate. Namibia celebrates him as a national hero because he has opened people's eyes to the ways in which a corrupt elite enriches itself.

Back in Iceland, people are uncertain what Fishrot means for the country. New whistleblowing laws have been met with scepticism.

In June 2021 the CEO of Samherji Thorsteinn Már Baldvinsson issued this apology: "It is my and Samherji's firm position that no criminal offences were committed in Namibia by companies on our behalf or their employees, apart from the conduct that the former managing director has directly confessed to and acknowledged. Nonetheless, as Samherji's top executive, I am responsible for allowing the business practices in Namibia to take place…I am very sorry that this happened, and I sincerely apologise to all those involved, both personally and on behalf of the company. Now it's important to ensure that nothing like this happens again. We will certainly strive for that."✕

Translated by **Shaun Whiteside**

Rainer Winters *is an expert on whistleblowing and the founding publisher of Ana Logo based in Kiel, Germany.*

50(02):66/68|DOI:10.1177/03064220211033797

Even though he issued bribes there himself, he has become something like the Robin Hood of Namibia

COMMENT

"By showing up to the protests, by standing up for each other, by rejecting the coup, we hope that we will one day get what we deserve – justice and equality"

FEMINIST ACTIVIST NANDAR ON BEING FORCED TO FLEE MYANMAR | A NIGHTMARE YOU CAN'T WAKE UP FROM P78

What is a woman?

Philosopher **KATHLEEN STOCK** argues that saying trans women are not women is a reasonable view to hold in the UK and should not be grounds for being sacked

MAYA FORSTATER'S APPEAL against a 2019 employment tribunal verdict has been decided in her favour. Tax expert Forstater originally brought the Center for Global Development to a tribunal in the UK after she had expressed certain beliefs on Twitter and been denied work by the CGD on that basis. The CGD had found those beliefs "offensive and exclusionary" and failed to renew her visiting fellowship. At the 2019 tribunal in London, Forstater's lawyers argued that this failure constituted discrimination on the grounds of philosophical belief, something prohibited under Section 10 of the Equality Act. But the judge, James Tayler, demurred, ruling that Forstater's beliefs failed to meet necessary tests for a "philosophical belief" technically defined in legal precedent – namely, they failed to be "worthy of respect in a democratic society" or compatible "with human dignity and fundamental rights of others". The tribunal found that her former employer had done nothing illegal.

The appeal in April – with the verdict to follow in the months to come – gave us a chance to revisit the particular beliefs at issue, apparently so shocking to Judge Tayler. Forstater believes that humans constitute a sexually dimorphic species, typically producing two differently sized and shaped beings, whose differently shaped gametes can then combine in the process of sexual reproduction. She believes that biological sex for humans is neither a feeling nor an identity but rather a lifelong material state that can't be changed through surgery, drugs nor anything else. She believes that

the capacity to refer, in language, to human biology and its various social impacts is especially important for one sex in particular: the female one, given the presence of sexism in society and divergent outcomes for the sexes in areas such as medicine, sport, employment and sexual assault statistics. Because of these beliefs, she also believes that she and others should be able to refer accurately to the sex of trans people in some relevant circumstances rather than be automatically forced to participate in a fiction according to which trans people have changed their sex to their preferred alternative. She professes herself politely willing to use preferred pronouns corresponding to inner feelings of gender identity but also wishes to describe trans women as biologically male in general terms – a description she believes is accurate – for the purposes of certain discussions of women's rights in practice. This seems to her

> She believes that biological sex for humans is neither a feeling nor an identity but rather a lifelong material state that can't be changed through surgery, drugs nor anything else

reasonable in a context where public policies about public spaces, resources and sporting activities are increasingly organised around gender identity rather than sex, with arguably serious consequences for women and girls. I'm an academic philosopher, employed at a British university. I share these beliefs of Forstater. Indeed, I'm about to publish a book defending them.

So when the tribunal judgment came out, it was more than a little worrying – if not also slightly comic – to discover that a judge thinks these beliefs of mine don't count as "philosophical" enough to gain basic legal protection. The judge was willing to concede that Forstater's beliefs – and so, presumably, mine – attained the required standard of "cogency, seriousness, coherence and importance", though he also suggested the beliefs were false, including the belief that there are only two sexes and that sex is immutable. This, he suggested, had been proven by modern science to be out of date. I think he's wrong about that and I explain why in my book. But either way, his opinion that Forstater is factually wrong is irrelevant as far as the judgment goes. It's not a requirement for protection under law that a belief seems true to a judge, nor even that there should be good evidence for it according to experts. Belief systems positively protected under Section 10 at previous employment tribunals have included Stoicism, Scottish nationalism, spiritualism and the belief that homosexuality is a sin.

The main basis for the original judgment seems to have been the assumption that stating beliefs about the sex of trans people – even in a generalised, third-person form – causes them "enormous pain", possibly even meeting the Equality Act's definition of harassment in some contexts, according to the judge. Forstater's appeal lawyers have argued that causing even grave offence doesn't meet the standard of harassment, and that the context of Forstater's statements shows they were not harassing. In their skeleton argument, her team points out that in a pluralist society with many competing perspectives jostling for space, the expression of views which cause offence to others is an inevitability. Hence offence on its own cannot reasonably be the grounds of illegality. They also argue, along lines originally suggested by John Stuart Mill, that "the taking of offence by one side … may indeed underline" the value of speech by the other side, since, where a challenge to a valued set of beliefs is particularly cogent and rationally compelling, there's a human tendency to compensate by moving towards defensive outrage in response. Citing multiple legal precedents, Forstater's lawyers stress that it's not a court's role to intervene on one side or another of any such contentious argument, except in extreme and exceptional cases where the aim is the grave destruction of the rights of others – something that is not the case for their client.

BY NOW, YOU might be wondering how has the expression of relatively mundane beliefs about biological classification – beliefs that even five years ago were uncontroversial and held by nearly everyone, and that still are held by millions of people worldwide – come to count for some, including for the tribunal judge, as approximating harassment? There are two plausible explanations: a narrow one and a wider one. The narrow explanation is highly efficient activist campaigning. Since 2015, the LGBT charity Stonewall has been advising organisations that an inner feeling of gender identity determines how you should be referred to in all

ABOVE: Two gender critical feminists protest at the launch of the UK's first transgender lingerie brand at Glazier's Hall in London, February 2019.

contexts, rather than actual facts about your sex, or even about your possession of a Gender Recognition Certificate if you are trans. Organisations pay to join Stonewall's Diversity Champion programme, whereupon they are instructed to replace references to biological or legal sex in policies and resources by inserting reference to gender identity or "self-ID" instead. These instructions have been heeded by many national organisations, despite neither the Gender Recognition Act 2004 nor the Equality Act 2010 concerning themselves with gender identity as a concept. Rather, these laws talk of "gender reassignment", legally identifying and protecting a process rather than a feeling. Even so, "misgendering" – that is, failing to "respect" a person's inner feelings of gender identity in verbal descriptions of them – has come to be understood

by many employers as automatically bullying and transphobic if done deliberately, and embarrassing and hurtful even if done inadvertently; something for which you should immediately apologise if you do it.

The influence of Stonewall in this respect extends to the justice system. Its Diversity Champion programme currently includes the Crown Prosecution Service, the Ministry of Justice, the Scottish Courts and Tribunals Service and a large number of police forces as members. The Equal Treatment Bench Book, produced by the Judicial College in order to guide judges in decision-making, also explicitly contains Stonewall recommendations scattered throughout. For instance, it advises: "Everyone is entitled to respect for their gender identity regardless of their legal gender status. It is important to respect a person's gender identity by using appropriate terms of address, names and pronouns." It adds: "It should be possible to recognise a person's gender identity and their →

He [the judge] also suggested the beliefs were false, including the belief that there are only two sexes and that sex is immutable

→ present name for nearly all court and tribunal purposes, regardless of whether they have obtained legal recognition of their gender by way of a Gender Recognition Certificate."

Leaving aside Stonewall's influence, a wider explanation of which the tribunal verdict is a prime example is an increasing tendency within society to elide the distinction between fact and value. As Forstater's appeal team pointed out, "statements such as 'woman means adult human female' or 'trans women are male' are (for her) statements of neutral fact not expressions of value judgment, still less of bigotry, transphobia or antipathy towards trans people". This interpretation is reasonable against a particular philosophical position on language generally, which says that in principle some sentences can be free of implied evaluations. They simply aim to represent and categorise what's already there in the world without assessing it positively or negatively. That is, there's a coherent distinction between description and evaluation. To say that trans women are male need not be a slur nor an insult nor a negative evaluation at all but rather could be, in context, a dispassionate description of a perceived fact about biological category membership.

These days, however, a rival theory of language is in the cultural ascendant. This says that any categorisation of humans automatically implies evaluation, no matter how putatively neutral its surface form. Statements of fact are always implicitly statements of value. On this view, to categorise someone as male or female is to implicitly set a normative standard which perniciously "excludes" and disvalues those who don't meet the standard. As the respondent's team described Forstater in court: "She is creating … a sort of sex superiority, which creates two classes of women: real and fake women. That is beyond the pale." On this view, then, concepts and categories such as "man" and "woman" should be made more "inclusive" on the grounds of social justice – just as if they were institutions or organisations seeking additional diversity in membership rather than shared cognitive tools whose whole point, arguably, is to exclusively identify certain kinds of people and not others, the better to refer to those kinds of people particularly in usefully fine-grained ways. In case it's not obvious, I think this second view of language is hopeless. But for as long as some bastardised version of it is floating about in the popular ether, we're likely to continue to see attempts by employers – and even perhaps by judges – to shut down discussion of perceived facts, on the grounds that they are supposedly automatically laden with negative consequences. ✖

Kathleen Stock is professor of philosophy at the University of Sussex in the UK

50(02):70/72|DOI: 10.1177/03064220211033798

The right to hold views "not akin to Nazism or totalitarianism"

SALLY GIMSON explains the Maya Forstater case and why an employment tribunal decided on appeal, she had the right to hold gender critical views

In the UK there is an increasingly polarised conversation going on about trans rights and women's rights.

It was triggered in part by proposals from the Conservative government three years ago for a gender recognition act, which would have made it much simpler for someone who wants to legally change their gender to do so. Currently in the UK, it can be a process which takes years, whereas in other European countries like Ireland, Norway and Portugal gender recognition is much easier. Harry Potter author JK Rowling published a long essay expressing her scepticism about relaxing gender recognition laws in the UK which ignited more debate.

This perhaps then explains the interest surrounding the case of Maya Forstater who has been given public support by Rowling. Forstater is a tax expert who enjoyed a fellowship with the Center for Global Development. She also has gender critical beliefs, ie that sex is immutable and not to be confused with gender identity. Her job and her beliefs collided when her fellowship was not renewed because colleagues complained about her views on gender issues which she had aired during debates on social media. Forstater took her former employers to an employment tribunal.

At a first hearing, a tribunal in 2019 decided that Forstater's views were "not worthy of respect in a democratic society" because Forstater would "refer to a person by the sex she considers appropriate even if it violates their dignity and/or creates an intimidating, hostile, degrading or offensive environment."

Forstater appealed this, arguing that her views were worthy of such respect. Index on Censorship agreed and acted as a so-called intervenor in the case. Index argued on

This is hate, not debate

PHOENIX ANDREWS says Maya Forstater has made the UK a more difficult place to be trans

DOES WHAT MAYA Forstater said in a series of tweets about trans women being men constitute hate speech?

That, for me, is the nub of the argument about whether she should have been allowed to keep her job or not. In the UK, under Section 4 of the Public Order Act 1986, language is criminalised if someone "(a) uses towards another person threatening, abusive or insulting words or behaviour, or (b) distributes or displays to another person any writing, sign or other visible representation which is threatening, abusive or insulting" if the target believes that language is intended to cause or provoke unlawful violence.

In relation to hate crime, the Crown Prosecution Service says: "There is no legal definition of hostility so we use the everyday understanding of the word, which includes ill-will, spite, contempt, prejudice, unfriendliness, antagonism, resentment and dislike."

As a trans person, I find Forstater's words to be abusive and insulting and at times threatening – at least in the abstract – towards large parts of the trans community in general. They are hostile, unfriendly and prejudiced and demonstrate antagonism, ill-will and dislike.

The trickier part is whether someone who sees or hears what she has to say believes it will cause or provoke unlawful violence. Indeed, the first employment tribunal judge ruled that what Forstater tweeted was not hate speech exactly but was "incompatible with human dignity and fundamental rights of others" and that her words did "not have the protected characteristic of philosophical belief" under the the Equality Act 2010.

As with many examples of offensive speech, people are going to argue about whether you can say what she said. However, it does not matter what most people think about what she said. It

matters what most trans people think, because we are the subject of her speech, and it matters that her words are part of a larger media and societal culture that is hostile to trans people.

Forstater's words do not stand in isolation. She is part of a network of "gender-critical" activists who collectively have made the UK a more difficult place in which to be openly trans.

I have experienced both physical and verbal violence on the street and in public toilets, and it has not always been from men. Violence from men is always the greatest threat to both cis and trans people. But incidences of bathroom policing and trans people being asked to leave toilets in public places or having their presence questioned have nearly always come from women.

The activism in which Forstater engages has made people who do not know her name or mine more wary of trans people. People understand how someone's words and actions contribute to wider hostility in the cases of other protected characteristics, such as race, faith, sex (not the transphobic dog whistle of "sex-based rights") or disability. They seem rather keener to argue the point when it comes to transphobia. They don't think their friends and allies can possibly be doing any harm to trans people just by saying things.

Forstater's speech is hate speech because of its contributions to the prevailing culture. The manifestations of her beliefs in speech and actions were also detrimental to the work environment at her former place of employment. Constantly voicing offensive views at work and on social media harmed her employer's reputation, and her co-workers, both →

strict free speech grounds that Forstater had a right to express and hold her gender critical views and they were protected under human rights legislation. So did the UK body which protects equal rights, the Equality and Human Rights Commission.

Forstater won her appeal. The tribunal concluded that her views were not "akin to Nazism or totalitarianism" which would have excluded them from protection under Articles 9 and 10 of the European Convention of Human Rights (ECHR). The three judges decided Forstater had "gender-critical beliefs,

which were widely shared, and which did not seek to destroy the rights of trans persons" and so "clearly did not fall into that category". The judges pointed out that this did not mean the tribunal had expressed a view in the trans rights debate; or that "those with gender-critical beliefs can 'misgender' trans persons with impunity"; or that transgender people did not have protections from harassment and discrimination; or that employers and services did not have an obligation to provide a safe environment for trans people.

CREDIT: Jessica Girvan / Alamy Stock Photo

LEFT: A protester at the start of Trans Pride in September 2020, Hyde Park, London.

→ trans and allies, had to work in an environment where they were not valued or treated with respect by Forstater. This manifestation continues to be harmful as she fights her cases and lawyers, journalists and commentators loudly defend her.

I have worked with people whose views I found offensive. Had they shared them in front of me or used their social media presence to attack minorities, I would have raised it with my employer, and I would expect any reasonable person to do so.

Index chief executive Ruth Smeeth's piece in The Times wants us to accept that "gender-critical" (anti-trans) views are "not the equivalent of race hate speech" and these are the grounds on which Index chose to intervene to protect Forstater's free speech. This pits one protected characteristic, that of race, against another, that of gender reassignment.

Many people think it is not as bad to say things that dehumanise trans people or make them feel miserable at work as it is to do the same for those whose skin is not white. The Equality Act 2010 makes clear that this is

manifestly untrue. There is no hierarchy of protected characteristics. By accepting that race, or any other kind of, hate speech exists, Smeeth has accepted that her definition of defensible free speech has red lines.

Most of us have red lines. Few people are true free speech absolutists, other than perhaps Noam Chomsky, who will happily sign letters of support for genocide defenders as well as for oppressed minorities, which at least is consistent. Gerrymandering those red lines to carve out exceptions for views you or people you respect happen to hold is not, however, a consistent defence of free speech. People seem more than happy to do this with anti-trans views. They're not just defending women and girls or just criticising ideology any more than anti-Semites are just making legitimate criticisms of Israel.

In a decent society, people committed to equality and inclusion should respect the characteristics and protections set out in the Equality Act and not seek to undermine ones that challenge their world view. This brings me to the power relations that are at the heart of

this "debate". I have put quote marks around that word because anti-trans activists constantly ask for a debate about trans rights, and they characterise the dominant trans position as No Debate. Prominent gender-critical professor Kathleen Stock promotes her new book using the hashtag "#YesItsADebate".

Are other protected characteristics a debate? Do we need to pit black women against white supremacists every week to check that black lives do, in fact, matter? Some broadcasters would argue that we should, but that's disingenuous nonsense. That is why we do not want to debate with people whose idea of debate is to crush a minority. It does not produce consensus: it wants trans people to admit defeat and not be allowed to use public toilets.

When Freeze Peach Live, a YouTube channel debating free speech in higher education and academic freedom, invited Stock to explain how she was silenced, she ignored the requests. Her views have been published all over the press with little to no dissent and her book has been reviewed by sympathetic journalists who espouse their own discomfort with what they call "gender ideology".

Gender-critical commentators, feminists and others (come on, now – Rod Liddle and Douglas Murray are not feminists) have created a moral panic about transgender lives and thrust us into a culture war while arguing that theirs is the grassroots position. Hundreds of thousands of pounds are raised every year in the UK by anti-trans campaigns hoping to crush us in the courts, and those campaigners get lavish support in the press as if they are plucky little grassroots efforts and as if the likes of Christian Concern and ADF do not have links to most of the cases.

LGB Alliance co-founder Ann Sinnott, a heterosexual woman, recently spent about £100,000 arguing that the UK's Equality and Human Rights Commission (EHRC) guidance on the Equality Act was wrong on trans inclusion. She lost the right to a judicial review, but she had a lot of support – including from Forstater.

There is no regular trans columnist in any mainstream newspaper or political magazine but there are plenty on the other side. Janice Turner writes dismissively about trans people every other week in The Times. Sonia Sodha writes leaders for The Observer and long Twitter threads about us. James Kirkup wrote anti-trans pieces for The Spectator more than 50 times in two years, plus multiple articles on the same topic for other publications. The think-tanks most popular with the government, Civitas and Policy Exchange, platform prominent people who hold anti-trans views.

There is only one regular trans ally columnist, cisgender man Owen Jones. There are no trans politicians in parliament. There are few trans councillors or university professors. Trans television presenters? No. All the money and power is on the gender-critical side. Even the EHRC's lawyer in Forstater's case, Karon Monaghan QC, has said she holds gender-critical views.

This "debate", as a result, has been defined by the gender-critical lobby, many of whom entered it as a result of the 2018 consultation on reforming the Gender Recognition Act, in relation to gender recognition certificates (GRCs). All a GRC does is change a person's legal sex and allow them to obtain a new birth certificate in the correct gender and to marry in the correct gender (so as not to have to suffer the indignity of being wrongly called a "husband" or "wife" in a ceremony that is meant to be joyous, and on subsequent paperwork).

Nobody can ever demand to see a GRC and you do not need one to change your name or gender on your passport or driving licence. It used to be expensive to obtain a GRC; the direct

cost has now dropped considerably (although not that of collecting all the evidence), but it remains time-consuming and bureaucratic.

The proposed change was that instead of collecting years of evidence and paying for medical reports that were then assessed by a panel they never met, a trans person could instead sign a statutory declaration of their gender and get a GRC. This is known as self-identification. The gender-critical turned this into a moral panic about "self-ID", meaning men pretending to be women and getting into women-only spaces that they couldn't enter before. GRCs, trans people in sport and puberty blockers for trans and questioning children are now the main battlegrounds for gender-critical activists.

Most trans people never bothered with GRCs due to the cost and hassle but also because they did not need them to live their lives. The Equality Act protects trans people without a requirement for medical treatment or a GRC, and changing most identity documents does not require them, either.

The issues trans campaigners are most exercised by are not GRCs, sport or puberty blockers. They are access to healthcare (which is currently near impossible for those who cannot afford to go privately), housing, protection from violence and dignity at work. Our time is wasted fighting to protect the rights we already have.

Gender-critical commentators, feminists and others have created a moral panic about transgender lives

There are two dominant liberal views that need to be challenged. The first is that debate is intrinsically valuable and desirable. The second is that free speech of the kind espoused by Forstater should be protected. Both these positions come from a Cold War liberal tradition where meritocracy is real, there are Reds under the bed, and debating societies produce more than insufferable thought experimenters in denial of structural oppressions.

This perhaps made sense in the days of Francis Fukuyama, when people believed that the end of history was real and all that developing countries needed to do was become liberal democracies with free and fair elections. However, that consensus has crumbled and citizens around the world have voted for populist leaders and campaigns that have horrified liberals. Debates that treat real lives as abstract issues have not helped at all. As for free speech, the liberals fighting for speech that is harmful to minorities do not experience its effects. I have heard some GPs refuse to refer trans people to gender clinics or prescribe medication recommended by endocrinologists under shared care agreements because, by their own admission, they are frightened of the Daily Mail and The Daily Telegraph. I have been lucky in the past that managers have understood the equality laws Forstater's demands challenge. But if she wins, who can I turn to when I am bullied by transphobic people at work?

Gender-critical activists give evidence in parliament and openly seek to take down charities such as Stonewall. Their words are cited in court cases in the UK and further afield. Speech is always more than just words. Fortater's win sets a precedent. It is a precedent that will harm trans people such as me. ✖

Phoenix Andrews is a writer and researcher. Their first book will be published by Atlantic in September 2022

50(02):73/75|DOI:10.1177/03064220211034451

CREDIT: (Abbad Yahya) Sharif Mosa; (graffiti) Godong / Alamy Stock Photo

Battle cries

Palestinian author **ABBAD YAHYA** talks about not being heard during the latest Palestinian-Israeli conflict

ABOVE: A wall of graffiti in a refugee camp near Ramallah, 2018. LEFT: Abbad Yahya

CAN'T REMEMBER THE first time I heard the slogan "No Voice is Louder than the Voice of the Intifada". I was born at the peak of the 1988 Intifada, when this slogan first appeared.

I became aware of it during the second uprising, when the slogan re-emerged at the start of the millennium. When I chose the topic of my dissertation – the impact of a prevalent ideology in determining the options of sociological research in Palestinian universities – I found that the slogan summarised how the existing national

ideology works against critical visions in social sciences and tries to silence them.

In my research I found that the slogan was a modification to one that existed during times of tyranny in Arab countries in the past century – "No Voice is Louder than the Voice of the Battle".

Ever since I was born, I've been living through the "battle" in which no other voice should prevail. This is what happens when you live in a conflict that has not been resolved for more than 70 years. I live in Ramallah in the West Bank, an area that is subject to Israeli

military occupation, according to the UN, since 1967. During this time there have been national movements working towards ending the occupation, but these have transformed into an authority that has signed a peace agreement with Israel that hasn't led to peace.

Instead, understandings were reached that resulted in administrative and security co-ordination. At various times, this has led to periods of calm, with economic opportunities and cultural activity which were supported internationally. It seemed as if the battle's voice had receded or faded away. Yet the administration maintained the battle discourse, which seemingly must remain above all others.

Years ago, on the wall of an oil

press in the village of my maternal grandparents, I read a slogan that shocked me: "You are either a mine that explodes under the feet of the enemy or you shut up." Underneath was the signature of a leftist faction. Reading this slogan, I realised that I was before two choices; I am either dead - because I am a mine that explodes under the enemy's feet - or I am muted.

In 2016, when I wrote my novel A Crime in Ramallah, I was subjected to a dual-pronged attack.

The first was a legal attack by the public prosecutor and the Palestinian Authority, who confiscated my novel from bookstores and libraries, issued an arrest warrant against me and detained the book distributor. The second attack was on social media, which fed on the prevalent ideology and its logic.

This incident highlighted the reality relating to freedom of speech in the areas controlled by the authority. Accusations were hurled at me about public morals and the current law, along with charges I had committed treason and insulted national symbols that are prevalent in the discourse of the "battle".

The current laws in force in the PA areas have remained a topic of legal argument. These include the penal code of 1960, which is a regressive law that restricts freedom of expression and speech as well as political freedoms, freedom of sexual orientation and the freedom of women. Furthermore, the law is vague and can be maliciously misinterpreted. The arrest warrant was issued against me on this basis. Efforts to amend the law or enact a contemporary law that allows for even minimal freedom of expression have all failed.

Instead, an electronic crimes law was issued in 2018. This further restricted freedom of the press and online expression. It included harsh penalties that had an impact on writers, journalists, artists and people who have now become hesitant to criticise the authorities even with a post or tweet on

Writers seem willing to sacrifice communication with the reader due to the fear of censorship

social media. Dozens of websites were blocked under that law, including a website whose editorial team I supervise.

Recently, major social media outlets have started censoring Palestinian content at an unprecedented level. As a result, I cannot write anything about the occupation and its practices in Arabic without the threat of my account being restricted or removed. Due to the weak algorithms of these sites in Arabic, the context is irrelevant – simply mentioning certain words is enough.

In an attempt that seems creative, social media users have begun to bypass the algorithms to avoid censorship by inserting symbols into words they think mean their accounts are restricted. Recently, this has evolved into a web application which removes the dots that are an integral part of Arabic letters, so that the AI machine cannot detect the words formed by them. This is interesting, bearing in mind that Arabic letters were originally dot-less 13 centuries ago. For a moment, everyone was happy with the ability to resist restrictions. However, I viewed this as a sort of normalisation with censorship, and I expected – along with many others – that these actions would succeed only as a form of protest. Clarity and freedom of expression are threatened because using such blurry letters hinders the communication process, which lies at the core of an open world and at the heart of these platforms.

This reminded me of writers, novelists and artists resorting to symbols to express what they want, using a sort of encrypted language. For example, they remove explicit statements in their stories and instead revert to a complex language that spares them the wrath of the censors.

It has become the norm to use symbolic language to talk about sex, cursing, politics and religion. Writers seem willing to sacrifice communication with the reader due to the fear of censorship. Actually, it seems to me that censorship has been internalised, evolving into deep-seated self-censorship, hence extensive symbolism in various genres, even in journalistic writing, is only expressive of an Arab censorship crisis.

Many thought that abandoning some words in my novel would have allowed it to escape the persecuting censorship, both officially and among the public. However, I believe that those words were a fundamental part of my style. I am also convinced that compromising on a few words means abandoning the basic right to write, and that whoever compromises on a word may compromise on an idea and then on an entire book.

Today, if I remain true to my conviction in regards to accuracy, clarity and freedom while writing on social media (which became a part of the "battle" through which I have lived my entire life) then I face two choices that remind me of the graffiti about the exploding mine: I either shut up or I cease to exist in cyberspace.

Finally, as I write these words, I am unable to express myself freely about the two sides of the "battle". I fear that many have surrendered to the fact that there is no voice above that voice, and I worry that I may be among them. ✖

Abbad Yahya is a Palestinian writer. His novel A Crime in Ramallah from which Index published an extract in 2018 was banned by the Palestinian National Authority

50(02):76/77|DOI:10.1177/03064220211033799

A nightmare you can't wake up from

Women's rights campaigner **NANDAR** writes about becoming a feminist activist in Myanmar and how the coup forced her to flee

ABOVE: Nandar taking part in demonstrations against the coup in Myanmar in 2021

WAS BORN IN a traditional Nepali household in a Shan State village in the north of Myanmar where "because you are a girl" is the reason to do or not to do something.

"Why do I have to help in the kitchen?" Because you are a girl. "Why can't I play with boy friends?" Because you are a girl.

So, I grew up with a lot of unanswered questions in my head such

as why don't my brothers do their dishes? Why can't I visit temples during my period? And why can't I go out after 6pm?

Like many teenage girls in my village, I had a goal to one day get married, have children and take care of my husband.

I heard somewhere that when you put a fish into a tank, it can only grow as the size to fit into the tank but if you put it into the ocean, it will freely grow as

much as it naturally does. I think it is the same with our brains.

Our brain is like a fish. If we live in a narrow-minded society where girls and boys are put into a box, we will think inside the box to try to fit in. Like the fish in the tank, I was trying to fit into the society I was raised in. I did all the things that are required to be a good girl, even though it was making me deeply unhappy.

I got a scholarship in 2014 that changed my life and my goals. In this social science programme,I learned for the first time that what we are socially conditioned to believe is not the only way to lead our lives. And that, as humans, we are born with rights that nobody – not the government, not even your family – can take away from you. My path to understanding my rights led me to activism.

It started when I stood up for myself and my rights to my family. I truly believe that just like violence begins at home, justice must also start from home. It was a long, ugly, slow process of making them trust me and my capacity to lead my life without their constant distrust or judgment over my gender.

I began my path to achieve financial independence by working in a local NGO as a teacher.

It felt like what Gloria Steinem meant when she wrote that "$50 that you earned gives you more strength than $500 dollars that others give you".

In 2017, after translating and publishing Why We Should All Be Feminists by Chimamanda Ngozi Adichie, my career took a turn from being a teacher to being a full-time activist. Through my writing and speaking, I actively became outspoken about the gender issues and cultural violence that women and girls have to face in my community.

Even though I had earned trust and support from my family, I started receiving harsh judgment and exclusion from my community. Many of them called me a "cultural ruiner" because

CREDIT: Umesh Puri; (right hand page) Phil Gribbon

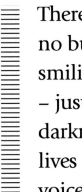

There is no music, no business, no smiling, no crying – just complete darkness with lost lives and unheard voices

I was challenging the harmful practice in the Nepali community in which menstruating girls are banned from their houses and prohibited to touch anything or go anywhere.

We call women who are bleeding "nah chu ne" – the literal translation is "untouchable". Our society fails to see this as a problem because their brains are like the fish in the tank. They do not get to grow.

With the help of the internet and the slow steps towards democracy, I was able to extend my work internationally by starting the Purple Feminists Group in 2018 to raise awareness about gender inequality in Myanmar.

I was also able to provide educational training and workshops to university students, teachers, government workers, doctors, lawyers and religious leaders to think critically about gender issues. Along with that, I ran two feminist podcasts with my team to amplify women's and girls' voices on topics including abortions, toxic relationships, menstruation, politics, domestic violence and more.

Then, right when we were starting to see a gradual but growing interest in feminism topics by the people of Myanmar, the coup occurred.

On Monday 1 February I woke up with no cell signal and quickly realised that something terrible had happened. I looked out into the street and saw many people were running and panic-buying. I needed some confirmation that what I thought happened had happened. I could not check the internet or call anyone to ask. I kept looking outside to get an answer, and saw military trucks playing the national anthem loudly and proudly to declare their success.

I felt devastated, angry, sad, helpless and hopeless, and I froze. Those feelings are complex and hard to process.

From that day, curfews were announced, fears were reinstalled, connections were cut, lives were lost and hope was diminished. That day can be marked as the beginning of living with the familiar fear with which our parents had lived.

As a feminist advocate who has been working in advancing the women's rights movement for years, it felt like the progress we had made collectively had just evaporated. I felt extremely demotivated to do any work. It felt pointless and meaningless to be doing anything about gender equity if the dictators were going to rule the country. And, realistically, if we continue doing it inside Myanmar, our lives will be taken away. So, I paused all the work that I was doing – producing the podcast, creating content and providing training.

I started joining the protests every day to show solidarity and because it was the only way to fuel our hope. By showing up to the protests, by standing up for each other, by rejecting the coup, we hope that we will one day get what we deserve – justice and equality.

Being disconnected from the world overnight is such a scary thing – especially when you have been connected for so long. The experience of living under the coup is like a nightmare that you cannot wake up from. It is like a storm that never stops. It is like an earthquake that destroys everything.

I returned to Yangon from Shan to work on relocating out of Myanmar. On my way back, the highway roads were filled with police and the military intimidating civilians. "Are you joining the civil disobedience movement?" "Are you doing anything illegal?"

What was more startling for me was to witness the sad, quiet, damaged Yangon. Yangon used to be a lively, fun and extremely busy city, especially at night. But now I see very few people walking outside, even in the daytime. There are no loudspeakers, there is no music, no business, no smiling, no crying – just complete darkness with lost lives and unheard voices.

Following the coup Myanmar has become a country that is hard to recognise as it used to be – peaceful and lively, yet complex, hardworking and beautiful.

We have lost more than 700 lives and there has been immeasurable suffering, yet we don't give up. The people who gave their lives for this aren't simply numbers.

Their lost lives will become scratches on the wall as proof that we fought, and are still fighting, back. The scratches will keep us and our voices alive even if we die. ✖

Nandar is a women's rights activist. She was forced to flee Myanmar after writing this piece but is safe and well in another country

50(02):78/79|DOI:10.1177/03064220211033800

ABOVE: Nandar at a performance in Myanmar in 2020

Trolled by the president

British journalist **MICHELA WRONG** reveals the storm of abuse she received at the hands of Rwanda's Twitter army

PUBLISH ANYTHING CRITICAL about the president of the tiny central African state of Rwanda, or his ruling Rwandan Patriotic Front (RPF) and you suddenly find yourself gazing into a freak-show mirror, where a ghoulish, unrecognisable reflection of your own face stares back.

In the weeks that followed the publication of Do Not Disturb, my fifth book on Africa, I wasn't surprised to learn I'd once been the mistress of Rwanda's murdered head of external intelligence: such smears are de rigueur for women reporters.

More intriguing was the notion I'd become best friends with his widow and had taken an oath alongside another "concubine", also a Western writer, to bring down the government in Kigali.

It was disconcerting to discover I'd always been a "genocide denier", since I have a vivid memory of reporting on Rwanda's grotesque national trauma for both Reuters and the BBC. Even more bewildering was the revelation I was a highly-paid agent for neighbouring Uganda. But what came as a total shock was the news I'd juggled my reporter's job with a role as spokeswoman for Operation Turquoise, France's controversial 1994 military operation in Rwanda. How on earth did I find the time?

All the above claims are, of course, scurrilous nonsense, put about not only by commentators and journalists employed by Rwanda's mainstream media, firmly under the government's heel, but by anonymous trolls of what is dubbed "the Rwandan Twitter Army", active across social media.

I'd never expected a warm reception in Kigali for Do Not Disturb. My book details the campaign president Paul Kagame has mounted to track down, harass, intimidate and assassinate opposition leaders, human rights activists and journalists both at home and abroad – a campaign to which Western governments have largely turned a blind eye. I expected a sharp response, but the crude malevolence has nonetheless proved sobering.

Once hailed as "visionary" by Tony Blair and as "one of the greatest leaders of our time" by Bill Clinton, Kagame has effectively been running Rwanda for 27 years now, and while development groups still wax lyrical about the government's performance on various fronts – its recent robust handling of the Covid crisis won much praise – human rights, including freedom of speech, have taken a terrible beating.

The constant monitoring and squashing of dissent or protest, both at home and abroad, are intrinsic to Kagame's modus operandi, an approach which can be traced to his roots as a young guerrilla in Yoweri Museveni's National Resistance Movement in Uganda. Kagame's first training was in military intelligence, and it left him with a deep appreciation for the dark arts of disinformation, fake news and rumour-mongering.

No African country is more conscious of its image, more defensive of its brand as a plucky post-genocide survivor run by a tough-but-inspirational taskmaster.

While the presidents of nearby Kenya and Uganda tend to shrug off criticism with a sigh, a hyper-sensitive Rwandan leader known for his attention to detail seems determined to control the narrative.

Despite its scant resources – Rwanda is the world's 12th poorest country – Kigali makes heavy use of PR companies in the USA and the UK who specialise in lobbying and brand promotion. At periodic intervals, details of their achingly expensive contracts are published on the internet by opposition activists. One of the interesting details that accidentally emerged during the ongoing trial in Kigali of former Hotel Rwanda manager Paul Rusesabagina was that Chelgate, a British public relations firm specialising in "reputation and relationship management", was coaching justice minister Johnston Busingye on how to handle awkward questions from the international press.

Such firms know how to bury coverage deemed insufficiently complimentary deep in the internet's bowels. A friend at a mainstream television channel tells me he's found it bafflingly difficult to locate an item he knew he'd recorded on Rwanda's 2017 presidential elections – polls which gave Kagame 98.79% of the vote.

On top of the corporate expertise, Rwanda can count for help on a group of Western academics and analysts who see themselves as custodians of the RPF's account of recent Rwandan history.

I wasn't surprised to learn I'd once been the mistress of Rwanda's murdered head of external intelligence

Quick to detect signs of sympathies for the Hutu extremists who committed the genocide, these "Friends of Rwanda" (as they are known in Kigali) regularly attempt to have critics no-platformed on the grounds of "genocide denial". In the process, they also stamp on questions raised by writers – such as me – who never doubt a genocide took place but who feel the RPF's appalling human rights record also requires attention. When Canadian journalist Judi Rever toured Europe in 2018 promoting In Praise of Blood, an attack on the RPF's past behaviour which lies at the extreme end of the spectrum, the Friends of Rwanda wrote to every university which had invited her to speak, urging cancellation.

MORE RECENTLY, 177 scholars and researchers signed an open letter demanding the University of Cambridge drop her from a panel event. In my case, Kagame's supporters resorted to launching an online petition calling on the Royal African Society to scrap a book launch event.

Domestically, the heavy lifting is done by Rwandan state employees and a network of amateur collaborators, working unpaid in the hope of eventual rewards and jobs. The National Intelligence and Security Services, the Directorate of Military Intelligence, the police and a unit within Kagame's presidential office run by his daughter Ange all communicate with a network of WhatsApp groups set up for the purpose.

I'm told the WhatsApp groups are each assigned target communities and specialise in, for example, Rwandan entrepreneurs, students or foreign commentators such as me. Members simultaneously run four or five accounts on Twitter, Facebook or Instagram.

"It's designed to look chaotic, a big mess, with lots of comments coming in from all directions, but in fact it's all carefully co-ordinated from the top," said one opposition activist based in London.

ABOVE: Former British Prime Minister Tony Blair with Rwandan president Paul Kagame in 2014 on a march to remember the Rwandan genocide of 1994

CREDIT: (Wrong) Kate Stanworth : (Blair/Kagame) Chip Somodevilla/Getty Images

I think I've learnt to spot the tell-tale signs of Rwandan intelligence-operated accounts. Sledgehammer insults are one giveaway: trolls don't usually waste too much time on reasoned argument. Other clues are the copy-and-pasting of accusations directly from one account to another, and the tiny number of followers: how many genuine Twitter users boast only 37 followers?

And then there's the strange dissonance between an account owner's supposed identity and the tweets' contents. "Look for detailed information of military operations when the moniker is a 20-year-old girl just out of uni," was the wry comment of one Rwandan analyst I know.

At best, the trolls hope to discredit and besmirch, counting on the human instinct which suggests that there's no smoke without fire. At the very least, they distract and demoralise while – crucially – sending out the message to any restive Rwandan citizen: "See what happens to anyone who puts their head above the parapet. Fancy some of this?"

The resulting cacophony conveys the impression of hundreds, possibly thousands, of irate citizens airing their views. The impression is misleading, though, when you consider that less than 5% of the Rwandan population is active on social media.

Once I'd grasped that what I was reading on Twitter and Facebook was a small group of hard-working propagandists, the jibes lost their sting. But the relentless vitriol of the Rwandan Twitter Army surely carries a message in itself for Western donors who support Kagame's government with taxpayer funds. Rwanda's inner circle has nothing but contempt for so many of the values dear to its foreign allies like freedom of speech and freedom of thought. ✖

Michela Wrong is a British journalist and author specialising in Africa. Do Not Disturb, her latest book, is published by Harper Collins

50(02):80/81|DOI:10.1177/03064220211033801

When the boot is on the other foot

RUTH SMEETH may not agree with what you say but she will fight every day for your right to say it

THE CONCEPT OF free speech must be one of the most challenged and debated of our core human rights. There are seemingly constant arguments about who has the right to say what, and where they can say it.

And that's even before you consider some of the more difficult issues such as misinformation, outright lies and political propaganda.

It should come as no surprise, then, that if you enter the term "free speech" into the Google news search function, more than 7.6 million articles appear.

Exploring issues such as academic freedom, freedom of expression, cancel culture, culture wars, misinformation, conspiracy theories, the role of social media and online speech, our collective right to free expression is constantly debated and scrutinised.

Of course, as chief executive of Index on Censorship, I don't just welcome this conversation, I celebrate it. I fundamentally believe that free speech as a human right should be cherished. But in order to do that it must be debated by every generation to see what we

really mean by the term and why it is important. This is even more crucial as technology advances and enables us to think and communicate beyond our own communities and cultures.

Every generation and political movement needs to embrace the concept on its own terms and apply it to its own battle and ideology. And those of us for whom the right to free speech is a core democratic right must be prepared to argue vociferously for it.

We must be able to make the argument that without our collective right to free speech and free expression, it won't be just the perceived "wrong-uns" who are silenced – it will be the trans activist, the feminist, the anti-racist, the politician, the pro-choice campaigner, the pacifist, the academic, the artist and the journalist.

You simply can't have free speech for the group of people you like and ban those that you don't – that isn't the way it works. It's free speech for all or you end up with free speech for no one.

But free speech, even at its broadest definition, doesn't include incitement to violence or extremism. It shouldn't, facilitate hate or empower extremists at the cost of undermining democratic norms. But what those norms are, and where the lines should be, is what we should regularly debate, because we have a fundamental responsibility to those people who don't have it: a responsibility to those people who have been killed in the fight for it; to those who live under repressive regimes and who must think twice about what they say, and to whom; to those who are

arrested for articulating their beliefs or doing their jobs as journalists or academics; and to those who cannot leave their homes without the fear that they won't return to their families because of what they have tweeted or painted – or even what they have taught.

According to the Economist's Democracy Index, more than 35% of the world's population currently live under an authoritarian regime.

They have no rights under Article 19 of the Universal Declaration of Human Rights – or at least they are afforded none by their own governments. Free speech is a dream, free expression a wish, and so many people around the world strive to achieve them every single day.

It is for them that Index was established in 1971. And it is for them that I fight every day for our collective rights to free speech and free expression, all around the world.

The team at Index proudly exists to be a voice for the persecuted, to publish their work, to shine a spotlight on their fights, and to be a small but determined beacon of hope for those who think the world has forgotten them. ✖

Ruth Smeeth is CEO of Index on Censorship

> ## You simply can't have free speech for the group of people you like and ban those that you don't

50(02):82/82|DOI:10.1177/03064220211033802

CREDIT: Gary Waters/Ikon Images

CULTURE

"Have I fallen behind the times fatally or am I one of the dwindling band of old fogeys who are still trying to hang on to the core truth of what freedom of expression means?"

PLAYWRIGHT TOM STOPPARD ON THE COMPLEXITIES OF MODERN LIFE AND WESTERN DEMOCRACY | UNCANCELLED P84

CREDIT: PjrTravel / Alamy

Uncancelled

SARAH SANDS interviews **TOM STOPPARD** and discusses
cancel culture, junk journalism and the dissident tradition

SOME CRITICS SPOTTED a finality about Leopoldstadt, Sir Tom Stoppard's play about generations of a cultured Viennese Jewish family charted through years of darkening anti-Semitism to the destiny of the camps.

LEFT: 'Leopoldstadt' at Wyndham's Theatre, London, 2020.

Jewishness, totalitarianism, history, family, enlightened conversation, liberty. It was as if all the cumulative themes of Stoppard's life were woven into this play.

The character of Leo, who escaped to England and led "a charmed life", is reproached by his cousin, an Auschwitz survivor: "You live as if without history, as if you throw no shadow behind you." If Leo is the self-portrait of Stoppard then the play seems to be laying ghosts to rest for a playwright in his 84th year.

This view underestimates the extraordinary intellectual curiosity and restlessness of Stoppard. Lockdown has been a time of productivity for him, although he has not yet found the subject of a next play. There are new subjects and there are perpetual themes. He is a champion of freedom and plurality against totalitarianism in all its forms. He joined the advisory board of Index on Censorship in 1978, after writing about the incarceration of the Soviet dissident Viktor Fainberg. His moral world view was forged by the Soviet tanks that rolled into Prague in August 1968 and his long friendship with the dissident writer and, later, president of Czechoslovakia Václav Havel.

The Jewish Czech émigré, bound like a sail to his past, is sitting in the kitchen of the rectory in Dorset that he shares with his third wife, the TV producer Sabrina Guinness. She has put the kettle on and is serving scones, jam and cream. Stoppard, who is sceptical of most orthodoxies, is chain-smoking.

We are here to discuss intellectual freedoms and his creative thinking, and he looks anxiously at my digital recorder and notebook. I remember the account in the recent major biography of Stoppard by Hermione Lee of a visit to his home by the former head of BBC Radio 4 to discuss a Reith lecture, only for Stoppard to talk himself out of the plan. His creative integrity is founded on

uncertainty and ambivalence; his choice of words is precise. Journalism can simplify and blunt.

Yet he retains a camaraderie and interest towards my trade, for he began his career as a reporter on the Western Daily Press in Bristol.

I ask him first about the creative catharsis of Leopoldstadt. Was this the completion of self? He says: "I didn't know how the play was going to develop and work out but what I did know was the last scene in the play would include someone much like me who came to England and had his name changed and carried on from there. I was nudged into it finally by a reference to myself in a book, Trieste by the Croatian novelist Daša Drndić. The heroine rebukes me – among others – for being too pleased with their luck and not looking back. I read this and my immediate thought was, 'she's right'. The seed for Leopoldstadt was planted in that moment, but I didn't know it. At the time I was obsessed with the problem of consciousness – 'the hard problem' – as it was known to neuroscientists – and until I'd written that play I wasn't open to anything else. Bloody typical! Set against my family history, consciousness was a problem? When I finally got to writing Leopoldstadt, it was an act of contrition to Drndić, but she had died a few months earlier. I wish I'd written to her."

Yet the scene became a smaller part of the whole and, as Stoppard points out, if he had wanted to make it entirely autobiographical, he would have made the family Czech rather than Viennese. →

Stoppard, the dramatist of ideas and pyrotechnic use of language, had chosen at last to confront his own history and identity. The late critic Kenneth Tynan had said many years before: "You must never forget that he is an émigré."

 Stoppard the man is the sum of his decades but he has a moral core of beliefs

The West's way of running a democracy is actually and intrinsically better

→ "I didn't identify personally with the family. Recently, I heard about somebody of my generation, my sort of background, whose name was changed in childhood, who because of seeing my play decided to revert to his original name. I mention that now because it never occurred to me to do that. I feel that I am the product of every decade of my life. I have been here for eight decades and I don't feel defined by my first one. I have become incrementally who I am from the age

of eight. I am now living an English life, with an English name and English attitudes. Because that is so, I am quite OK in my skin, to be this person. I don't need to see myself differently as a result of this play."

Stoppard the man is the sum of his decades but he has a moral core of beliefs. He fled from the tyranny of Nazi-occupied Czechoslovakia as a child and confronted the Soviet tyranny that followed. He wrote in 1985: "We must still retain the view that the Western way of attempting to run a democracy is absolutely and metaphysically better than the undemocratic systems, not just because of some emotional preference for the system but because it is actually and intrinsically better."

Is this still the case? The West now has to deal with the forces of populism, the internet and a rise of orthodoxies such as cancel culture which might

threaten the tenet of free expression. Stoppard is too intellectually honest and curious to be complacent about his lifelong principles.

He draws on a cigarette, both handsome and frail. He talks of a lessening of energy to write and to think and yet he is as alert as a hare.

"What I was about to say was that essentially my views pretty much remain where I was when I was taking a proper interest in what was happening before the late '80s when the Soviet Union existed, and it seemed absolutely clear to me that free expression was what made all the other freedom possible, so it was everything.

"I am not sure that I feel very different now, and we will come to whether the existence of the internet only alters the rules or changes the game. The view I took was that if someone indulges their right to free

ABOVE: Left to right. Playright Arthur Miller, Stoppard's friend and former Czech president Václav Havel, then president of PEN International Ronald Harwood and Stoppard himself. Pictured in 1994.

expression by putting forward a truly anti-social argument the only response was to put a better argument. I'd have to stop and think to know whether I am still there." He pauses. "Yes. I am."

A test of his resolve was the journalistic practices uncovered by the Leveson Inquiry, which in 2011 and 2012 investigated the culture, practices and ethics of the press in the UK. He tried to stand by his mantra that "junk journalism is the evidence of a society that has got at least one thing right, that there should be nobody with the power to dictate where responsible journalism begins". He has kept fragments of coverage from that era, parliamentary reports, responses.

"I believe in a free press. I support Hacked Off because I want a free press to be a fair press which comes clean about its mistakes. Self-regulation failed and continues to fail. I'm on a knife-edge about regulation. When I read about some egregious behaviour by a newspaper, my blood boils and the idea of some kind of legislated redress for the victim no longer seems like anathema. But when I read about online investigators Bellingcat or listen to the podcast of the Paul Foot award for investigative journalism, I have the opposite reaction – hands off at all costs, even the cost of whatever unfairness. Journalism is fractal, it won't separate into segments. Leveson was 10 years ago now; day after day, free expression in the context of British journalism seemed to me to be about as important a subject for any kind of writing, including plays, as you would find. But I never got as far as understanding how to deal with it as a playwright. Theatre is a storytelling art, and I didn't know how to tell the story."

More testing is the tornado of information on the internet and the new frontier of cyber warfare. Can the better argument be heard in the storm of "alternative facts"? How does contemporary public discourse feel to someone who values truth and precision above all?

His shoulder stoops slightly. "It feels ungovernable. And I don't know what to do about it. A line of Philip Larkin comes into my head: 'Get out as early as you can and don't have any kids yourself'.

"It's a kind of funk, it's a kind of relief that the big problems will be somebody else's, starting with climate change. So like most people I know, I try to do my bit on the side of right and the side of good behaviour and the right way to live, but that feels like making a posture towards a world that hasn't arrived yet and looks as if it will arrive after I have gone. So I feel a bit cowardly about that – I mean, too passive."

Then, cheering himself up, he adds: " I have always been good at zig-zagging. I have always got a zag to my zig. Theatre is recreation. Entertaining is worth the effort, adds a bit to the common good. So there are these conflicting thoughts in my mind."

What captivates him more than politics and current affairs is moral philosophy. "What is the good life? The questions that interest me enough for me to want to write a play about them are unfortunately so generalised across human behaviour, human nature, that you end up saying nothing about a real-life problem."

His cuttings about a free press are the nearest he has got to preparation for a play. He always returns to the prevailing theme of his adulthood: freedom of expression.

"Have I fallen behind the times fatally or am I one of the dwindling band of old fogeys who are still trying to hang on to the core truth of what freedom of expression means? Since I am an old fogey, I naturally hang on to that."

What does freedom of expression mean to Stoppard in these times?

"My utopia is an arena where it is not just two sides of an argument, it is every side. A pluralism in which every side is free to express itself. I would pretty much have no problem with even the excesses of an over-excited popular press if the corrective to a particular excess was

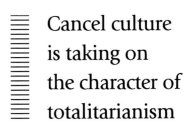

Cancel culture is taking on the character of totalitarianism

freely heard in the same arena."

Is the pluralism of the internet compatible with this utopia or does social media drum out pluralism?

Stoppard replies that he is "attracted to the cacophony of the market place". He likes the idea of the Hyde Park Corner soapbox as an electronic platform. But he asks: "Can a Hyde Park orator represent what is free? It is so asymmetrical. Now with the internet, the equation is just as unwritable as in mathematics, the equation is out of control."

He defines censorship as "getting ahead of publication", and this is the most worrying threat he sees to freedom of expression. It is the closing down of thought. It is the culture of cancellation. "What worries me is that the way the conflict is played out feels like the orthodoxy of those societies I was fighting against. The society which is now accommodating to the cancellation culture is taking on the character of totalitarianism. Of course, it is not totalitarianism, it is a different kind of frenzy. Both of them – the orthodoxy of totalitarianism and the orthodoxy of wokeness – take on the characterisation which one remembers from Stalinist and Maoist society. A kind of contagion. It is really quite ironic how the big battalions of corporate and commercial enterprises capitulate to the first murmurings of what is now the new demotic player.

"The other night I got to the end of an 800-page biography of Philip Roth I read a bit of Philip Roth 'back then' and more recently. It would be difficult to find another writer who is as illuminating as a spokesman for a certain part of American life. ➔

→ "In other words, it is a book worth writing and a book worth reading and it is good that somebody wrote it and did a good job. And anybody who cares about writing should care about the absolute freedom to publish a biography of somebody like Philip Roth.

"And the idea that a really rich big publisher like Norton should throw in the towel at the first inkling of alleged misbehaviour by its author is astonishing."

The publisher, WW Norton and Company, cancelled Roth's biography, halted the distribution of unshipped copies and cut ties with its author Blake Bailey because of allegations of sexual harassment and assault. Bailey has denied any wrongdoing.

"It feels like a big defeat for literary culture," says Stoppard. "In saying what I am saying about the book, I am not taking a view on the personal character of the biographer or of the subject of his biography. I am taking a view on the freedom to write and read the book.

"So you catch me at a moment in which I am quite depressed that the publisher would rather pulp 50,000 copies of this book rather than being willing to defend publication for fear of appearing to be underwriting somebody's alleged behaviour. One doesn't want a world where one is spuriously made to feel that one is taking sides on the wrong question."

The appeal to judge writers for their work is surprisingly controversial in these times. Censorship is a cultural issue. Cancellation is coming from culture and, as Stoppard puts it, "culture determines everything".

He adds: "Back then we used the term 'brainwashing' a lot. We used to think of millions of Chinese waving Mao's Little Red Book as people who had been brainwashed. It shared some characteristics of a religious fervour."

I ask Stoppard about the nature of this cultural orthodoxy. The swiftness to condemn perceived transgression could be belief akin to religion – or could it be commercial self-interest? I ask him for his analysis, for instance, of the ditching of author JK Rowling by the cast who owe their fame and fortune to her.

He responds thoughtfully: "I asked myself at the time and since whether Emma Watson and Daniel Radcliffe acted from self-interest and panic, or whether I am really so far out of it that I can't make the imaginative leap into the head of someone who was authentically affronted by what Rowling said.

"I have now got grandchildren, and I think this is a truth for them. Whereas I come from a generation where there seemed to be very little argument about what truth meant."

I quote Oprah Winfrey talking to Meghan Markle about "her truth". Is truth now assumed to be subjective, rooted in identity? How does it sound to a playwright who has spent his life trying to define the meaning of words, and thus their truth?

He shakes his head. "I would love to be able to write something, anything, which would make Meghan stop in her tracks and say: 'Oh my God, I get it. Thanks Tom!'"

Was he sympathetic to the response of the Queen that "recollections may vary"? "It only increased my admiration for the Queen," he says.

Righteous certitude seems some distance from the "cacophony of the market place" which is Stoppard's intellectual forum. Is there room for doubt in our contemporary culture? "I threaten to see very often both sides of an argument. So I was very responsive to that period of Oxford philosophy which was essentially saying that anything not only true but intelligible had to be verifiable. That was my understanding about meaningful propositions. You can say that Virginia Woolf was the fourth tallest novelist in Sussex but you can't say that she is the third best. It has to be verifiable."

Are universities still a place for free thought and questions?

"God, if there is anywhere where truth should be up for examination that's where. The whole thing of 'my truth' just feels wrong. In a totalitarian society, for example, you can have Marxist physics, or capitalist physics. The idea that truth is susceptible to a view that is relative was and is still so wrong-headed to me it seems hardly worth contradicting it. It is bewildering, actually.The danger to society of actual censorship has probably never been greater. "

Stoppard, who has written of putting on Englishness "like a coat" and has defended this island democracy against angrier anti-establishment writers, sounds unexpectedly fretful and sombre.

"It could not have occurred to me in the 1960s, '70s, '80s, '90s that this bulwark would begin to give way. It is deeply worrying because my position has always depended on people in general in this country holding, broadly speaking, common sensical views. It was other kinds of ideologies, other kinds of societies where the defences had given way. I used to say to myself that the difference was that abuses in Britain – and there were many: police corruption, whatever – were examples of a failure in the system, whereas in an undemocratic society, the abuses – violations of human rights – were an example of the system in good working order. That was a make-or-break frontier for me. That was the fault line between a fair and an unfair society. Now one asks oneself, can one actually say that all the abuses are the failure of the system or have they

CREDIT: Liba Taylor / Alamy

'I'm on a knife-edge about press regulation. When I read about some egregious behaviour by a newspaper, my blood boils'

ABOVE: Tom Stoppard in Prague in 2009

insidiously become part of the system? You have to ask yourself if you are being naive or if there is something substantial which has gone missing, been corroded."

He is reluctant to be too particular but names the Greensill Capital lobbying affair in the UK as one example. The day after I see him, the story breaks about journalistic deceit at the BBC's flagship Panorama programme 25 years ago.

Does the "moral chasm" between the West and the communist world still hold true to him? Stoppard answers a more profound question. What were Václav Havel and his fellow writers fighting for?

"They were not trying to bring about a consumer society. They didn't want Czechoslovakia to go from being communist to being West Germany. They were more idealistic about the kind of democracy they would have. Because of larger forces beyond my ability to delineate, the broad tendency has been towards a kind of populism. I think driven not so much by ideology as by a realisation that capitalism can itself be distorted for self-enrichment."

The wind is whipping against the kitchen window and rain comes as if in handfuls of stones. Stoppard is incapable of intellectual complacency but his view of the world outside these solid rectory walls sounds more than questioning: it sounds sorrowful.

I ask him about religious thoughts and he describes himself as "not practising, nor irreligious". Then he perks up. "I am told that very few people in the scientific field nowadays think there is such a thing as free will, whereas I do. I feel strongly that free will is a real thing."

He pauses and we grin at each other. "It is a brilliant subject," I say. "Yes, that is a good example of the kind of thing which unfortunately appeals to me as a possible play..." ✖

Sarah Sands is chair of the G7's Gender Equality Advisory Council and a board member of Index on Censorship

50(02):84/89|DOI:10.1177/03064220211033803

'Extremely important
and profoundly disturbing'
ARCHBISHOP DESMOND TUTU

**Do
Not
Disturb**

The Story of
a Political Murder
and an African
Regime Gone Bad

MICHELA WRONG

'A withering assault on the
murderous Rwandan regime
of Paul Kagame – very driven,
very impassioned'
JOHN LE CARRÉ

'An extremely important and
profoundly disturbing book'
ARCHBISHOP
DESMOND TUTU

'A withering assault on the murderous regime of Kagame,
and a melancholy love song to the last dreams
of the African Great Lakes'
JOHN LE CARRÉ

LEFT: Photo-journalist Hayat al-Sharif is known for her portraits of Yemeni women

No light at the end of the tunnel

BENJAMIN LYNCH introduces Yemeni author **BUSHRA AL-MAQTARI** and photographer **HAYAT AL-SHARIF**

NOVELIST AND ACTIVIST Bushra al-Maqtari campaigned against censorship for many years. Born in 1979 and raised in the restrictive societies of Saudi Arabia and Yemen, she is one of the standout female literary voices from the latter.

Her debut novel, Behind the Sun, was written in 2012 and released to critical acclaim. She won the Françoise Giroud Award for Defence of Freedom and Liberties a year later but her work has never yet been translated into English.

The book, an extract from which we are publishing below, reflects on Yemen's fall into the mire of civil war and the world's worst humanitarian crisis. It details how glorious revolution developed into grim disillusion, where women appear as little more than an irritant.

For other women writers in Yemen, al-Maqtari, who is currently being treated for a brain tumour, is an example of courage in the face of a world that doesn't approve of what they do.

She told the German broadcaster Deutsche Welle that Yemen was where "her writer's soul belongs" and she did not want to alienate her country by leaving. She has created a large body of work including books which document the testimony of victims of war.

When al-Maqtari won the Johann Philipp Palm Award for Freedom of Speech and the Press in 2020, her friend Monika Bolliger, a Der Spiegel writer, said: "Bushra's writing is a refusal to give in. I hope that she will continue to be that voice that is a thorn in the side of tyrants and war criminals."

Al-Maqtari is not the only one determined to carry on, even though female activists and journalists are constantly held back.

Houthi-controlled Sana'a is particularly restrictive. The Houthis, who now control most of the Yemeni population, are a theocratic Shia force akin to the regime in Iran, which is their biggest backer.

Photo-journalist Hayat al-Sharif is based there, and she explained that a combination of a lack of education and condemnation of female voices meant women writers were "aggressively fought".

"Yemen has a very high illiteracy rate and the people here are linked to customs and traditions that prohibit women from working," she said. "Women are not allowed to speak or write on social or political issues. The society is aggressively fighting women's work. Writing in Yemen is considered a crime by the authorities, and by the society that is subordinate to the authorities. The ➔

> For other women writers in Yemen, al-Maqtari is an example of courage in the face of a world that doesn't approve of what they do

→ corrupt use force against the writer – you are not allowed to write, take pictures or speak."

Barriers to writing and reporting are numerous and al-Sharif must apply to each of the four local authorities for permission to carry out her work.

Should this be denied, she would be actively defying the state that frowns upon a woman carrying out her occupation.

"As a photo-journalist in a war-torn country, I have suffered between my work and the four powers – the Sana'a authority, the Marib authority, the Aden authority and the coalition authority. In order to film a project I must obtain permission from everyone. This is very difficult."

The Yemeni civil war has raged for nearly seven years. The longer it continues, the worse the humanitarian disaster will get and the harder it will be for Yemeni women to speak out.

An end to the war is not likely to bring relief, either. The Houthis will not provide Yemeni women with the ability to express themselves. They are in a tunnel with no light in sight. ✖

Benjamin Lynch is editorial assistant and Tim Hetherington journalism fellow at Index

50(02):91/94|DOI:10.1177/03064220211033804

Behind the Sun

By Bushra al-Maqtari

I ASKED THEM NOT to send me back to Saada.

"Didn't you run away, soldier? With your tail between your legs? Leaving us exposed? As if you get a say in the matter now!"

No words came out, my hands slick with sweat.

"You've been blacklisted, Yahya," my superior continued, slipping the report into my file.

Whenever I think about what he wrote in that 500-page report, crammed with black text from top to bottom, scribbles falling out of the margins, I feel my heart in my mouth. All my dedication, my struggle, my love for the nation: all of it hidden from the committee's eyes. Reading the camp commander's damning statement, my throat tightened, the military penal code a cleaver dangling over my head.

"It wasn't like that, sir!" I cried out. My superior officer didn't answer, and in the closed proceedings of the military court I sat crouched, a guilty child in the lawyer's shadow. Five years in military prison. Case closed. My record scrubbed clean. Sign here, Yahya. I signed the papers and returned to my duties at the prison clinic with a filthy black file.

God, those Saada war years are all anyone talks about. They said jump. I said how high? And now, with the anniversary of their victory coming, I've got to stand up for what I did. I can feel their eyes boring into me; keep your ears open, Yahya, listen up. My superior officer left the room, leaving me alone with my demons. Stuffing my mouth with khat, I focused on making my breathing more deliberate. When is Abbas's night shift again? I need a break. But the power's been out for some time, and I'm afraid to go back to our neighborhood, a battlefield between the Dawa' men and the youth. Ever since I've been living here, I've been avoiding those Muslim preachers as much as I can, but sometimes they'd greet me and I'd respond warmly; they'd ask about how things were, meaning with me, and I'd say everything's well, brothers. They'd ask our names, which mosques we pray in, and if we chew khat before praying or after. I'd answer patiently, yes, we chew khat with our wives and sometimes at work to keep loneliness at bay. At night they grow rowdy, threatening the young men sitting in the vacant lot watching TV, passing round joints. "Why are you all sitting out here?" they'd ask. "Why don't you go on inside?" A sarcastic quip or two would result in blows. A few weeks ago, their group showed up in their shortened white trousers and thick beards, led by bulldozers. My neighbor Mohammed yelled from his window, "They're coming! Should we go outside or turn off the lights?"

"Turn off the lights," I said. "It's got nothing to do with us."

But my wife wanted to throw me into the fire. "Go on, Yahya," she urged. "Aren't you a soldier?"

"What am I supposed to do? The police are

already dealing with it, don't you see the squad lights across the street? And look, our aqil, too, he's standing right there." Our neighbour's voice was cut off suddenly. I heard his footsteps outside, women's shrieks mingled with exclamations of "Allahu Akbar!" I watched as bulldozers tore down Muhsin Allawzi's home. Furniture smashed to pieces on the street, children crying and women sobbing on the stairs. Eyes staring out from windows, watching what was happening, as I did the same. But what matters is that it didn't happen to me. The Dawa' men set off down one of the alleys with Muhsin, who had been gripped by silence like so many other things.

I went back to bed. "Come here, woman, come closer." My wife threw me a dirty look. Silence. Yahya can't even control his own home. How I hate this woman. Since when has she hated me? I keep a gun under my pillow. A soldier's got to be on his toes these days, you never know what's in store. "Get over here, now," I told her. "I'll give it to you like they did Muhsin." She paid me no mind, like I wasn't even there. After I beat her, she tried to run away. I locked the door, pocketing the key. You'll get over it in a few days. But she never did.

Don't you know you're my legal property? I can have my way with you whenever the hell I want – it's my right. Damn you and damn the way this marriage has rotted away my soul. What do I care about your life? What matters is that you came to me as a virgin.

That day the men from my tribe gathered, their gunfire ringing out in the neighbourhood. I sang Ayoub's wedding ballad, it always moved me deeply whenever I heard it at other weddings. I sing the wedding song from our old house. It's not the same house now, not the same life. I sing, thinking of that distant night.

The sheen of my tribe's eyes remained fixed on their rifles. I was the cocky groom on his first night. You laughed at me, and I laughed too. That was the last time we laughed together, before we grew to hate one another. A miserable husband, a stubborn wife, your head always in the clouds pouring resentment onto me. Why is this woman such a stranger to me? Be patient, Yahya, I told myself, this depression will go away on its own,

but you grew even more distant, and now when I get a sense of the scale of your hatred, it blinds me. I come home late from work and find you reading. Who gave you that book? Why don't you answer? I don't seem to exist for you. I feel a lump in my throat when I look at the woman living in my house. The woman I coldly have sex with, why don't you come to me for once, then we can both apologise and make up? Everybody has another face, it's like Yusuf said. Is everybody dead and I'm the only one who's alive? No, I'm not alive. Everything inside of me was dead before you came with your suitcase into this house. I put my hand on my heart and I feel the coldness of death, like the bodies I saw, the bodies I killed, the bodies hidden under my skin.

Why don't you draw near to me? I need to sleep and forget my combat boots, my helmet, my file, my years of service. Forget the prison clinic and Yusuf. For some time now we've stopped recording what he says. Before, we used to write daily reports: his movements, his visitors, his words, and sometimes I'd get fed up with writing, but my superior would say, "He's the leader of a cell."

"Which cell, sir?"

"A Marxist group that's threatening the country."

I'd asked him, what does Marxist mean to us here?

"Atheist, you idiot. You want to be an officer with lots of stars on your shoulders? With a car, and hands saluting when you go past?"

"Yes, yes, I do, sir. I've been waiting for that moment since the day I first wore this badge on my shoulder."

Write, Yahya, and don't get tired, keep writing, Yahya, and don't ask questions. For days on end, I wrote down everything he said and everything he didn't say. Had he gotten better? Could he write? Did they give him a pen? No pen. No paper. He could be planning something. Write, Yahya. Today he spoke of some people, said they're from his generation, and it'll be the same tomorrow: the same talk, the same names, the same books. I got tired of him, just like everyone else did, and left him alone.   ➜

→ For the past few weeks the Dawa' men have been turning their attention to a new battle, marrying off underage girls. They gathered their Korans and camped outside Parliament, surrounding it. The images of them broadcast by the news channels, in their eyesore threadbare clothes, were chilling, but isn't religion all we've got left? What do you want, darling, would you rather go back to your religion? They'll make you choose, and maybe they'll burn your face with nitric acid, but why do you let every passerby see your face at all? Your face that's become an insult to me on the street and at work, they're saying Yahya can't control his woman, while I choke on my long rope of rage. My rage that you don't know the first thing about.

You're just a soldier, Yahya. How I hate the word when you say it, it's only then that I really know how much you hate me. Or even "Askur", like our neighbour Mohammed calls me. Sometimes names like "little soldier" annoy me, and I don't know what to make of them: and sometimes, I'm pleased, remembering the soldier I used to be; at others, I just want to scrape the label off with a knife, but it's forever stuck to my skin. I told myself, extend an olive branch to her, try to see her side of things. But your thoughts are dark, wife of mine, I know this, and I know that all those who are like me get whipped by your barbed tongue. You say I hate soldiers. I'm afraid that one day I might wake up and not see your resentful face next to me.

I got up from where I was and went to look for Yusuf. I found him leaning against the wall. I lit a candle for him and brought him a chair, saying, "Have a seat Yusuf, you'll get tired of going round and round." He mumbled and made his way to the window. I fetched him some water. "Have you had your medicine?" He swore while I just stood there. He gathered up the chairs and placed them in a circle. Then he sat in the middle with his hands held high, looking at me; we exchanged looks and he smiled.

"Why are you smiling at me?" he said. "I never smile at you." Who the hell was he smiling at, then? Annoyed, I went back to my bag of khat.

Khat wasn't giving me the energy or motivation today that it usually did. I'd been up since early this morning, woken by the racket of the nurses in the clinic corridors. The senior officer was pacing in the courtyard. Seeing him made me remember my black file. I gulped.

"There's an electroshock session going on," Dr Saeed informed me, and I excused myself. I always avoided anything that could take me back to that glass-panelled room. Years ago I'd witnessed an electroshock session like that. It was March and it had been pouring since the crack of dawn. Muddy water on the ward floors and the public squares, the whole world cloudy. The doctor asked me to restrain the patient stuffed into the room. A very young man, barely more than a child, really, who I still think about. What made you go crazy, son? Did someone bewitch you, a stepmother perhaps, or one of your "friends"? Did you lose your mind because you saw the children coming back from there, limbs without faces, their families sobbing while some cold-blooded officer tells them, "They're the martyrs we need." I spoke to the patient, his cloudy eyes first directed at me but then drop to the floor empty, like our soldiers in Saada. The boy smiled with a simplemindedness that frightened me. Seeing me perplexed, the doctor said, "Secure him, Yahya." I grabbed him by the hands and held him back against the chair. The doctor pressed the button and the boy convulsed. Oh, you dear boy... Be strong for your mother, she's right there behind the glass in tears, just imagine you're a boy like everyone else. While I spoke to him, the boy's eyes bulged and his body began to shake even more violently. Stronger than all of us. For a fleeting moment he looked off in one direction, as if at the opening in a door ajar, smiled at his mother, and his flame was extinguished forever. ✖

Translated by Sawad Hussain

Bushra al-Maqtari is an acclaimed Yemeni author and winner of Johann Philipp Palm Award for Freedom of Speech and the Press in 2020

Dead poets' society

The Myanmar military is detaining and killing the country's poets. **MARK FRARY** speaks to
KO KO THETT about two fellow writers who have been murdered during the country's bloody coup

SINCE 1 FEBRUARY, when Myanmar's Tatmadaw military force seized control of the country from the democratically elected government of Aung San Suu Kyi's NLD, the blood has not stopped flowing.

The UN called 3 March "the bloodiest day" of the coup so far.

UN special envoy Christine Schraner Burgener said that, on that day, 38 people had died in protests against the actions of the military and its commander-in-chief Min Aung Hlaing.

The blood that has flowed has included young and old, journalists and taxi drivers, singers and artists. Yet the country's poets have, perhaps, had more of their blood spilled than any other group.

Among the dead on 3 March was 38-year-old poet K Za Win, from the township of Monywa.

On 21 February, the poet whose real name was Chan Thar Swe shared what may have been a premonition in a Facebook post. "Even if you and I are apart, I will sacrifice my life for you," he wrote. Less than two weeks later, he was dead at the hands of the Tatmadaw. K Za Win was no stranger to protest and had spent a year in jail for taking part in a student rally calling for reforms of the education system.

On 9 May, the family of Khet Thi – an antagonist of the military regime and and member with K Za Win of the Monywa poetry circle – announced that he, too, had died and his body had been returned with its vital organs missing. The poet had been taken in for interrogation by armed soldiers just the day before.

These two are not the only ones to have died since 1 February: U Sein Win and Myint Soe have also perished at the hands of the Tatmadaw. Many more are in jail, where torture is commonplace.

In memory of the two poets, who

ABOVE: (left) The poet K Za Win before his death in March; (right) Khet Thi died after being taken for interrogation by Myanmar's security forces.

were widely published in Myanmar, and in support of the others who have been detained and tortured, Index has asked fellow poet Ko Thett, who knew both K Za Win and Khet Thi, to translate a poem from each into English. These are published here for the first time.

Thett said: "Both Khet Thi and K Za Win were prominent members of the Monywa poetry circle. As a poetry translator and anthologist, I am always after exciting poets. I met Khet Thi in Monywa when I returned to Myanmar in February 2014. In 2015 my girlfriend and I ended up visiting his family home... a memory I will always cherish. →

 "Myanmar probably has the highest poet population density on earth"

"I came to know K Za Win only when I translated his poem A Letter from a Jail Cell in January this year. There is a long tradition of poetry in the country. Myanmar probably has the highest poet population density on earth," said Thett. "[But] poets like Khet Thi and K Za Win, who have dedicated their lives to poetry, may be few and far between simply because it's not possible to make a living out of poetry in Myanmar."

Thett says the theme of injustice was at the heart of both poets' work.

"Both are native to the lands west of the River Chindwin, but they have very different family backgrounds. Khet Thi belongs to a relatively well-to-do family who own a peanut oil press and K Za Win to a dispossessed peasant family whose farmlands were grabbed by a Chinese mining corporation," he said.

"Both of them may be called witness poets – poets who witnessed the political transition of Myanmar. The transition and its accompanying economic and social injustice were often their subjects."

Thett believes that the reason poets have been targeted is clear. "Unlike politicians, poets are hardly rational," he says. "True poets are untameable." ✖

Mark Frary is associate editor at Index

50(02):95/99|DOI:10.1177/03064220211033805

A letter from a caveman

By Khet Thi, for Ko Than Tun

Exhausted with a front crawl across hell
I hitched a speedboat ride.
I had no idea
my shortcutism would sink me even faster.
I patted my lap
I shot up in the air
I kneed the firmament.
I thought I was fab.
I had no idea
when hubris slapped me in the nape
I would have to hang my head.
Even when falling topsy-turvy
from a high wire
I flew a fly kiss to my fans —
I was a circus act.
I had no idea
real friends have to be panned like gold
in dukkha.
Now I know
antidepressants
don't really cure the downhearted.
You can't put out a fire in your chest
by fleeing into fuel.
In the last-ditch fight with my own shadow
if I can't kill it, I know, it will kill me.
I dig through the depths of an abyss
to give myself an introspection.

I find my body and soul ablaze.
If not for metta,
I would have been reduced to ashes.
Where are you?
Where are you?
I look for myself.
Forced to prescribe a meaning to my own existence,
Ethic equals Empathy is what I've learned.
Just for a moment,
The burden cable tends to snap quite often.
Just for a moment,
I am still changing the burden cable.
I will be back.
Heroically, I will be back.
Not a hero who will knee the heavens in the groin,
the hero who will kneel down
to kiss the earth.
When we meet again
won't you repress "Nice seeing you again."
with your usual sardonic smile;
"About you we haven't any tattle." ✖

Khet Thi was a former engineer and poet who died while in military custody a few weeks after Ka Za Win was killed

Translated by Ko Thett

Translator's note: The poem is dedicated to the influential Monywa poet Ko Than Tun, a former political prisoner and a Myanmar National Literature Award laureate.

The clarion call of a rainbow

By Ka Z Win

Right now,
to my country and parents,
and to that young lady
I am in love with,
I am a rainbow
ensnared on the horizon.

In this country
during the dark days that
gang-rape us,
like a warrior off to war
brandishing a dah
I am out in the street
with my dah poem.

I am fearless.
I am fussy.
I am firm.
I am unsteady.

Like a crocodile
I've crawled,
my chest firm on the earth.
Like an ape
I've hopped from one branch to another,
only to grab the air.

In this country
where the majority is filthy poor
and a minority is filthy-rich
it gives me no pleasure
to be a patriot.
No pleasure
to love my parents.
No pleasure
to fall for that young lady.

None of my prayers,
nor playing with myself,
gives me pleasure.

Like weed that grows
in the tundra
I've come of age.
I look back at myself,
my country and
my friends
for over thirty years.

From the Buddha
and pongyis
to panhandlers
I look back at all of them.

Everywhere I look
I see fish in the fish traps.

I can't help, but see
the welt of dukkha,
the Noble Truth,
festering with pus and blood.

I can't see
our own faces.

The rainbow that's gone haywire
has given up their identity.
So have I.

I've learned
to oppose pagoda donors,
whose names are inscribed in stone.
It is the masses
who lay bricks for their pagodas.

I've learned to
hurl fuck-yous at
the army and the affluent
who ride both the left and right shoulders of
my land
when I am tipsy.

What else can I do?

→

→ On such a spacious land
our humanness is limited.
Our rights are limited.
Our freedom is limited.

Our landscapes
do not go beyond the hills,
stationed with snipers.
Limits are everywhere.

And still
our people through the ages
have bored through unjust limits.
They have bored through the pages.
They have bored through the classrooms.
They have bored through the factories.
They have bored through the paddies.
They have bored through the roads!

Parents
who've bored through
won't be home for their children.

Children
who have bored through
won't be home for their parents.

Students
who have bored through
won't come back to classrooms.

Labourers
who have bored through
won't return to their carving knives and chisels.

Peasants
who have bored through
won't return to their ploughs.

People on the street
who have bored through
have bored through the depths of an abyss and
will never return.

Blood
breaks out at every corner.

In the Age of Bankruptcy
no wonder
our beliefs have gone bankrupt.

No wonder the arahatta daza,
the banner of the sangha,
the saffron robe of the monks,
stamped flat under the army boots
on an asphalt road prays,
"Long live the President."

The demon Mara,
who has stolen the Buddha for fifty years,
waves the sword of evil in fits of delirium
until his very last breath.

The machine of the ignoble
foams at the mouth.

O the Most Noble King,
He who is blessed to become the future Buddha,
He who has kicked in the face of the Metta Sutta,
don't you dare touch my country
with your dirty hands!
I, the poet in chains, command you!

"Fear makes
injustice feel at home."
Rise, mates, rise,
let's bore through the blood-thirst
of despotism.
Let's bore through it again.

Let's embark on a long march.
Let's march again.

Let's yank the failed state
out of the not-so-funny gags of the politicians.
The tongues of their gaungbaungs
flap shamelessly in the air!
Let's yank it out again!

Just like the loggers who
will cut the branches of a tree
before felling it, let's put on trial first
the two nefarious classes
behind the Mara mechanism.

To see a rabbit out of a hat
we put up with the mumbo jumbo
of the magician for over fifty years.
In the end we let that rabbit
guard our carrot farm.
Years and years were wasted.

Down with congenital authoritarianism.
The despot is decomposing alive.
The fish-saucy smell of his rotten corpse
stinks to high heaven all over the country.

Spring fruits
in the orchard of the insane
are infected with worms and maggots
before the harvest.

Our war is no longer
a war against a foe that we can eliminate like a foe.
Our foe is pretending to be our friend;
the hands that have killed the sangha
are building many a stupa.

As the Buddha prophesied,
"udakamanyay ardatetan …",
water is on fire.

O the venerable, the Vexillum of the Nation,
you might be able to forgive the jackboots
who have trampled on your shaven heads.
No matter what, could you please
not leave the Buddha's words,
"ma pamar datta beikkawai…",
under those boots.

C'mon, mates!
Let's exorcise
the evil spirit that has
possessed our land.

There is a long dark night
between the dawn of democracy
and the dusk of despotism, a time when you can't tell
your blood brothers from strangers.
Let's ring our bell to that truth.

C'mon, mates!
Let's wake from the nightmare,
the nightmare gifted to us by
those who possess us.

Let's set fire
to the fake spring
that refuses to obey orders
from the people.

Take out the tainted flesh
from the feast of the people
and bury it for good.

Set the revolution alight,
let us be as brave as Prometheus,
let's sacrifice ourselves!

C'mon, mates!
Resist the devilish
temptations.

Like Spartiates
at the Battle of Thermopylae
let's get rid of defeatism,
let's make a last stand.

The way we hold on to our swords,
let's hold on to our blood-red creed.

To my country and
my parents,
to the young lady I love,
and to my friends,
I send my untethered love,
wrapped in a poem,
like a clarion call from a god.

O people
the day has arrived!
It's time you
enhance your sumptuous feast
with justice flavour! ✖

Ka Za Win was a Burmese poet and former Buddhist monk who was killed by the military in Monywa in March 2021

FOR EVERYONE WHO WANTS TO UNDERSTAND 'CANCEL CULTURE'

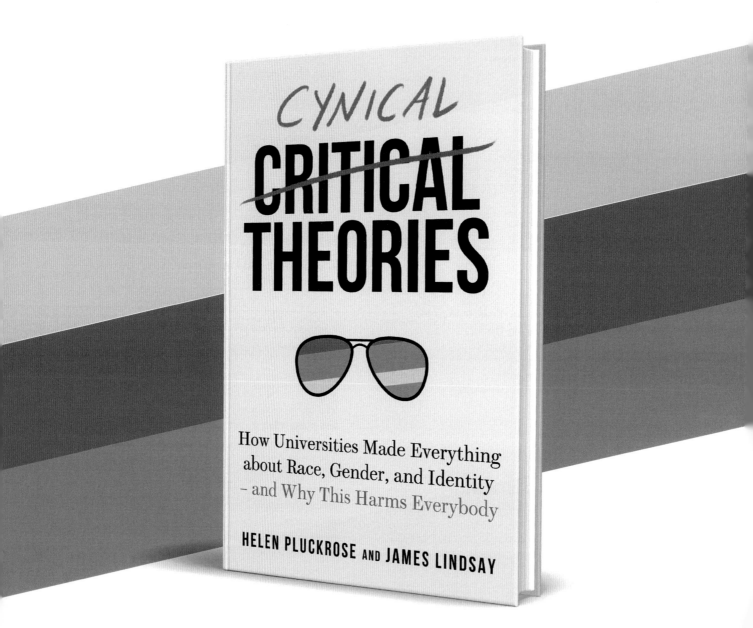

Cynical

~~CRITICAL~~
THEORIES

How Universities Made Everything
about Race, Gender, and Identity
– and Why This Harms Everybody

HELEN PLUCKROSE AND JAMES LINDSAY

BOOK OF THE YEAR

The Times | Sunday Times | Financial Times

'Brilliant' *Daily Telegraph*

Swift

Politics or passion?

MARK GLANVILLE introduces the American poet STANLEY MOSS, who has an abiding love of China

ABOVE: Zhou Enlai, the vice chairman of the Chinese Communist Party, recieves a delegation in 1967. The blackboard shows a poem written by Mao, in his own handwriting.

"**Y**OU'VE GOT A lot of poems on China," Michael Schmidt, the boss of Carcaner Press, remarked to Stanley Moss. "Why don't you put them together?"

Not Yet, Moss's new collection is the result. At a time when China draws attention chiefly for its threat to Western interests, oppression of the Uighurs and as the source of the Covid-19 pandemic, Moss's poetic Sinophilia, based on long experience of the country and its culture, is refreshing.

Its opening poem, Preface, recounts the development of this affection, from the seven-year-old who answered a teacher telling her class "You wouldn't want a Chinaman living next door to you" with "Oh yes I would!" to the 62-year-old invited by the poet Willis Barnstone to teach in Beijing.

A number of poems in Not Yet are paeans to Alexander Fu, the child of Chinese friends who lived with Moss and worked for his New York art-dealing and publishing companies.

Moss's connection to Chinese people and poetry is deep.

"Of all the foreign poets who have read to us, Stanley Moss's poetry is the most Chinese," claimed students of the poet and translator Fu Hao. According to Hao, in his afterword, Chinese poetical tropes such as

"family, friendship and even emotional connection with pets are recurrent themes in Moss's poetry".

Yet the poet and Sinologist Willis Barnstone, in his foreword, claims that "Stanley sees all in a political frame". Who is right?

"Yehuda Amichai once said 'All poems are political'," said Moss. "There was a programme for him at Yale, and somebody said 'Oh, but he doesn't really write much about the Holocaust' and I got up and said 'Poetry isn't just what it's about. It's what it's informed with'. All Yehuda's poems, including his love poems, are informed by the Holocaust."

Describing the genesis of the poem, Murder, he suggests that "a highly civilised" Chinese lady's curious decision

to vote for Trump was influenced by her child's experience of being imprisoned, under Mao, in a room with 25 other people. "They were given food once a day, which was shoved through the door, and all the defecation came out once a day." Trump's opponents were too socialist for her.

Moss was once a Mao supporter, principally because Mao's opponent, Chiang Kai-shek, was pro-Nazi.

Murder was inspired by a trip to China, where Moss was shown a poem Mao had written in calligraphy. "Such a great poet," remarked his guide, even though her own husband had been killed during the Cultural Revolution.

In it, Moss lists poets with dubious beliefs: Ezra Pound the Fascist, Pablo Neruda the Stalinist – drumbeaters rather than statesmen.

"I asked [Neruda] if he would sign a petition to get [Soviet dissident Andrei] Sinyavsky out of jail and he said no."

Personal experience informs Moss's →

I write when I have things that I don't understand

→ A Prayer to No God for Ilhan Comak – the Kurdish poet who is one of Turkish president Recip Tayyip Erdoğan's many prisoners of conscience.

"Have you ever spent a night in jail?" Moss asks. "I have… I was in a cell with two other people and I realised a cell is a toilet. If you're in a cell with somebody, you're locked in a toilet for 27 years."

Approaching 96, Moss is at his most fertile and prolific. In old age, he claims with authority, "some people get even better".

Perhaps the affront of Trump has played a part. For Moss, an atheist who sees God(s) in everything, Trump, enabler of racists and bigots, is an anti-God. In his 2016 poem Trump (not included in this collection), Moss writes: "Our Father who art in Trump Tower / hallowed be thy portfolio / thy casino come, thy will be done / in real estate as it is in Heaven."

"They say you write when you have something to say," he said. "I write when I have things that I don't understand and, in the course of writing about it, I understand it a little better. It's a big, big, big difference." ✘

Mark Glanville is a writer and singer. His memoir, The Goldberg Variations, was short-listed for the Wingate Prize for Jewish Literature and his band Amaraterra will release their first album later this year

50(02):101/103|DOI:10.1177/03064220211033806

Moss was once a Mao supporter, principally because Mao's opponent, Chiang Kai-shek, was pro-Nazi

A Prayer to No God for Ilhan Comak

Almighty, please give some pleasure
to a Kurdish poet, prisoner, student of geography,
locked in a Turkish cell for 27 years.
I hope his cell has a window so he can see
birds, trees of some kind, occasionally
a human being, the beauty of the world.
Does he know in English, God and prison guard
sound the same? Does Allah, a prison guard, whip him?
I bless you, Lord, I'll hear your confession.
May Ilhan tell stories with happy endings
to himself. He remembers very well
the smell of good cooking. He knows a man
can be locked in his cell with his love locked out,
still the good ghost of his love lies with him
on the toilet cell floor decorated
with flowery dead defecation.
I hope he can pretend he's having good times
swimming across the Bosphorus to Asia.
Saviour, give him hope if he has no hope,
give him children, a dog, a cat, toys,
the world, an imaginary toy he can play with.

Erdoğan's gang is against it, but the poet retains
the freedom to speak to himself,
play with himself, sing to himself,
argue with himself in Kurdish.
If giving up his principles freed him,
I think he'd refuse dirty silence.
After 27 years in a cell, would I shut up?
In prison without hearing loved
music or new music,
except your own songs and whistles, is torture,
an upside-down crucifixion.
I wish hell were a real place for Erdoğan's mob
a place where they are all equals, so they
have the pleasure of living with themselves.
Can Ilhan read books, the Quran, now?
In the Kurdish geography of his cell,
there is Syria, the Red and Black Seas.
From my farm in Rhinebeck, New York,
in the Catskill Mountains, near the Hudson,
across the world, a man who never prays
writes this prayer for him.
I'm his friend he never met,
a Jew he will never meet.
Free, I believe Ilhan would fight to the death
for his countrymen, Kurds without a country,
live for the right to tell and write the truth,
sometimes called kindness, sometimes poetry.

Murder

The great poet murderer Chairman Mao
wrote nothing like an evolutionary sonnet
in calligraphy. Forever, then, and now
even if you can't read it, his poetry is beautiful.
After the Long March the great famine came,
people ate less than rats, blood was champagne.
Mao Zedong was milk, the one tit
that allowed the infant China to exist.
Mao's first wife was mentally ill, he said,
"I'll make her a sane, happy communist."
He sent her to Moscow for ten red,
red years, Mao's favorite colour, not the green
green that Lorca loved. Mao let temples
stand, but he cut off the heads of Buddhas.
He could write a poem beautifully simple,
a gift with a Little Red Book to the people
the same day murder a village of do-gooders.
I paint good news on a krater, neither fake;
the word poetry comes from the Greek to make,
the Chinese character is to keep.
A rattlesnake, I want to make and keep.

* * *

I thought of murdering a lady
who was destroying my son, the reason
I sent her roses wrapped in poison ivy.
April. T.S. Eliot dedicated The Waste Land
to *il miglior fabbro* Ezra Pound.
With breeding lilacs in hand
Pound cheered, raved for Mussolini.
He wished all the Jews were gassed
in death camps. In the end he repented,
he pitied himself, he said his life was a mistake.
There were great poet meanies,
Neruda was a kind Stalinist, alas.
There was one Jorge Luis Borges,
one Paul Celan, one Seamus Heaney.
The ship of life is sinking, poetry is a lifeboat,
wintery death murders, poets give us an overcoat.
Roethke was a racist. I don't see Theodore
waltzing at lynchings. (I see anti-Semites galore,
from the empire state's cellar to the top floor.)
Will Burroughs, writer, "gunshot painter," shot

his wife dead, both of them on H and pot.
I believe in the very right and very wrong,
not sin. Nothing is worse than murdering,
I've heard someone murdering a song.
There's still an electric chair at Sing Sing,
I had a distant cousin who sat in it,
a poet did not throw the switch.
Anyway, the Lord was mistaken to think
"I'll murder" is the same as doing it.
I'm going uphill, I'll never reach the summit.
I sew a poem together stitch by stitch.
Camels pass through the eye of a needle,
the devil plays hymns on a fiddle.
The days of our years are threescore and ten,
rich men get more years than poor men.

* * *

I cannot forget great poet and murderer Mao
not soon or after, now,
disguised, I will sip his cup of tea.
I will stir every line with the spoon, "kill."
Kill. I is a dangerous word. Never forget
Kill. the pronoun *we* confiscates private property.
Kill. Alone, Mao's ideas are not private property.
Kill. Dine with two people, three can't keep a secret.
Kill. One child take care. If you beget
Kill. a girl, should you want to keep her, you have a debt,
Kill. you owe a son to the people's army.
Kill. A puppy sandwich tastes better than salami.
Kill. Peasants and factory workers know by heart
Kill. the poetry of Tu Fu.
Kill. Buddhist death is a work of art.
Kill. I still want poetry that "makes it new."
Kill. Suffering and grief are teachers.
Kill. if life were cinema, life's one reel
Kill. life is not a double feature.
Kill. Be civil, run away from evil,
Kill. beware of the white peril. ✖

Stanley Moss is an American poet and the founder of
Sheep Meadow press

END NOTE

Are we becoming Hungary-lite?

JOLYON RUBINSTEIN fears a British legislative agenda that could stifle protest, satire and the very foundations of democracy

PICTURE THE SCENE.
I'm driving a pick-up truck. I'm dressed in a high-vis jacket and white overalls and in the back is a tonne of manure. On the side of the pick-up is the logo "BS Industries UK". We drive up to and block the front entrance to the Houses of Parliament, immediately drawing a bevy of armed police officers (or, as I like to call them, "supporting artists") towards us.

"You can't park here!"

I explain that this is "Grade A bullshit" and that "the MPs ran out of bullshit so they need a fresh batch to feed to the public".

The prank, filmed in 2013 as part of the promotional campaign for the second series of our Bafta-winning BBC show The Revolution Will Be Televised, was an expression of that quintessentially British tradition of using satire as a tool of protest. Creative direct action dressed up as a comedy sketch, if you will.

For me there is nothing more British than using satire that laughs at the powerful, and that in a very minor way holds the powerful to account. But under clause 59 of the Police, Crime, Sentencing and Courts Bill which is going through the UK parliament now public nuisance is being criminalised and I could get 10 years in jail for such a prank! Ten. Years. In. Jail. I know that's not the funniest joke but come on…!

History teaches us that things don't change if the status quo is not disrupted and the intention appears to be to create an environment where you can make a lot

of noise, as long as you stay in your lane, but where any movement deemed effective at changing hearts and minds and making a real difference is criminalised.

The passing of the PCSB in Parliament signals an active attack on this cornerstone of British democracy. Perhaps the significance of it is that freedom to speak truth to power without the fear of recrimination or criminal sanction is a British value as well as being a fundamental tenet of freedom of speech!

What does it feel like when the democracy you grew up in starts a gradual slide towards authoritarianism? Perhaps patriotism and flag-waving replace public debate. Perhaps the very fabric of public life starts to warp and change so that rational argument about policy is replaced by questions about how many national flags were printed on said policy paper. Perhaps the worse the state of the nation becomes, the more national greatness is invoked.

But what of those who question this new status quo? In societies where the ruling class wallows in corruption and enjoys total impunity, its enemies are a free press, and those who protest are criminalised. I'm not saying we are suddenly Myanmar. I'm not saying we are even Hungary. But maybe we are becoming Hungary-lite.

In a letter to the government in March co-ordinated by Liberty and Friends of the Earth, 245 organisations said the government's proposals were cause for "profound concern". The organisations highlighted numerous threats to our rights, including

ABOVE: Jolyon Rubinstein addressing a crowd outside Downing Street in 2016.

"draconian" police powers to restrict protests. The signatories represented a wide range of interests from Amnesty International to the Ramblers.

Hundreds of mainstream charities as well as groups such as Sisters Uncut, All Black Lives UK and Reclaim the Streets have committed to building a mass movement to resist the bill. But its protest and public order provisions could result in this very movement having its actions disproportionately criminalised for participating in peaceful activity. Even former prime minister Theresa May has voiced concerns over the proposed bill, insisting that the government has to walk a fine line between being "popular and populist", and telling lawmakers that "our freedoms depend on it".

It seems pertinent to ask if any amount of protest will be enough to stop the bill passing into law? The proposed law is indicative of a slide towards authoritarianism deeply at odds with the founding principles and traditions of the ruling Conservative party in the UK, and the democratic principles that many of us in the oldest democracy in the world hold so dear. ✖

Jolyon Rubinstein is a British actor, writer, producer and director

50(02):104/104|DOI:10.1177/03064220211033807

CREDIT: Johnny Armstead/ Alamy Live News